GW00394098

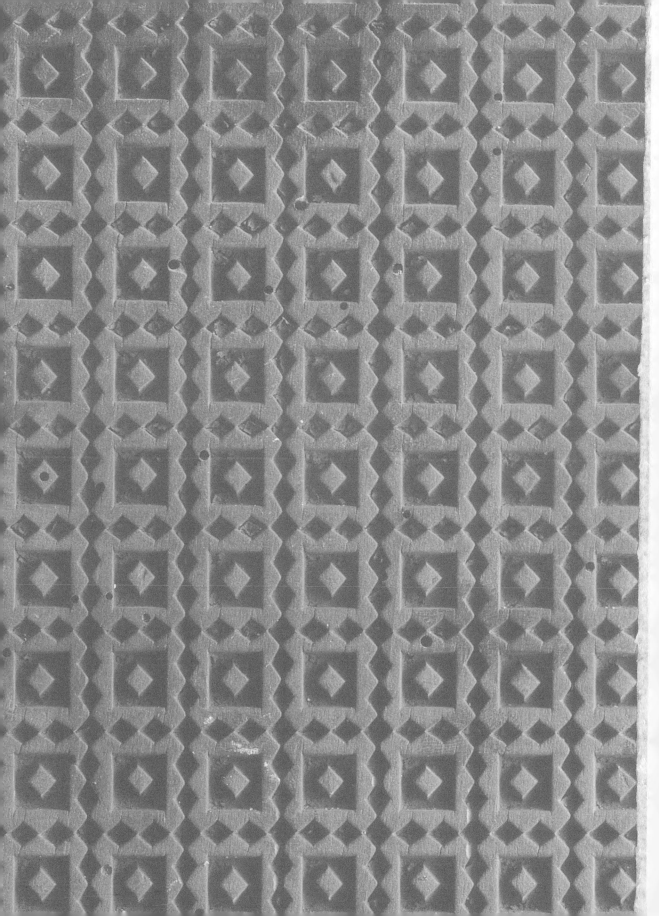

FRENCH
STYLE AND
DECORATION

Thames & Hudson

FRENCH STYLE AND DECORATION

A SOURCEBOOK OF ORIGINAL DESIGNS

*with over 600 designs, patterns and settings
in colour and black-and-white.*

STAFFORD CLIFF

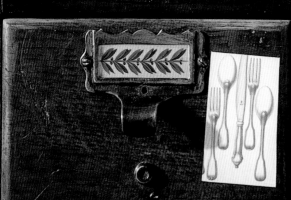

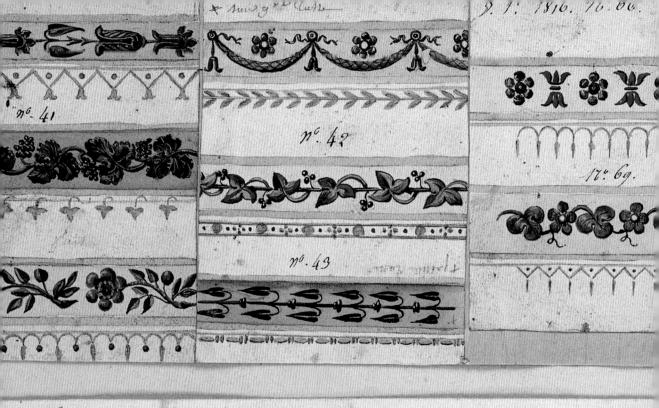

n°. 41

n°. 42

n°. 43

N°. 69.

D. 4. 1817. N.º 13. (Huard.)

no. 35

no. 66

no. 38

no. 36

no. 67

no. 39

D. J. 4. année 1817. No. 21. (Huard.)

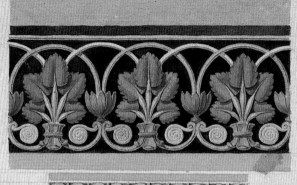

Glaïeul (Selby)

AUTHOR'S
PREFACE

Hidden in the archives of museums and manufacturers in towns and cities throughout France are published and unpublished records and original designs which testify to the astounding richness of the applied arts, from the age of Versailles to the nineteen-thirties. Like its companion, *English Style and Decoration*, this book is not intended as a formal history of the decorative arts of a nation but, rather, as a glorious celebration of a unique heritage, created by designers and craftsmen both known and unknown.

Here, for instance, are pages from company archives and pattern books which display dazzling virtuosity, yet many of the creators of these supremely beautiful designs have remained anonymous; here, too, are pages from some of the most famous pattern books, portfolios and published works of the period, displaying the creations of the known designers who made French artefacts pre-eminent in every European market for luxury goods.

I have sought to achieve a balance between these two groups within each of the period sub-divisions, to convey the great wealth of a design culture which has always been at the very centre of national self-esteem. Indeed, the decision to begin the book in the latter part of the seventeenth century was partly inspired by the fact that Louis XIV deliberately and consciously decreed in various ways that the decorative arts should be central to the national interest and a means of maintaining the prestige of France abroad.

Whatever the origin of the designs illustrated, humble or illustrious, they have been chosen because of their ingenuity and intrinsic beauty, and because their appeal is as great today as when they reflected immediately the fashions of the time in which they were drawn or painted. Wherever possible, I have tried to show initial designs and sketches, rather than later printed renderings. The result, I hope, is an anthology brimming with creative energy, the images as immediate and vital as if they had been done yesterday.

INTRODUCTION

From the seventeenth century onwards, from the Ancien Régime to the great decorative arts exhibition of 1925, the design and manufacture of finely crafted goods have been central concerns of successive political régimes in France. In their encouragement of excellence in the creative and technical aspects of the decorative arts, the monarchies and Republics of the last three hundred years affected an attitude towards the applied arts which was pretty well unique to France: that achievement of the highest order in the making of the fine things of gracious living was, somehow, a sign of a wider national well-being which could be directly orchestrated from the centre of political and social influence.

Thus, the terms for successive styles and fashions are often synonymous with the holders or styles of power: Louis-Quatorze, Régence, Louis-Quinze, Louis-Seize, Empire and Second Empire. And in Republican France, the great international exhibitions held in Paris helped to define the major styles of the late nineteenth and early twentieth centuries: Art Nouveau, Art Deco and International Modernism.

Such concern with the decorative arts also brought economic benefits. French styles became known throughout Europe during the eighteenth century for their elegance and distinction; they were imitated from Spain and Portugal to the capitals of eastern Europe. Even London had a flirtation with a form of Rococo in the mid eighteenth century. And with the export of styles went the export of artefacts; the silks, porcelain, furniture and silver produced by the great French manufactories and the master-craftsmen of Paris came to be recognized every-

where as being the finest money could buy. Inevitably, too, such promotion of the nation's luxury crafts and industries was accompanied by a constant flow of published pattern books, catalogues and records. Such publications – along with original company design archives – are the visual subject-matter of this book.

There is a kind of official quality about many of the French pattern books, as though their designers, engravers and publishers were recording examples of the national genius. Under Louis XIV there was a highly centralized effort to promote a distinctly French style – one which was effectively a celebration of the brilliance of the court of Versailles. The appointment of Colbert as Surintendant des Bâtiments in 1664 – a sort of prototype Minister of Culture – was indicative of the king's intention to make the development of the decorative arts a matter of royal and therefore national pride. In 1667 the status of the manufactory of Gobelins, on the outskirts of Paris, was elevated to that of Manufacture Royale des Meubles and placed under the control of Charles Le Brun, by now painter to the king but formerly the principal influence on the design of Vaux-le-Vicomte, the château of the former Surintendant des Finances, Nicolas Fouquet. It was to be Le Brun's responsibility to create a national style which would be seen to best advantage in the palace of Versailles, where the court was installed in 1682. From 1685 Louis decreed that all new furniture designs for royal residences should be entered in the *Journal du Garde-Meubles*, thereby recording the definitive style of the time. About the same period those designer-craftsmen most closely associated with Le Brun and the Gobelins, notably Jean Le Pautre (1618–82) and Jean Bérain (1638–1711), who was himself an engraver, began to publish collections of designs, spreading the French court style throughout the French provinces and further afield. Le Pautre alone was responsible for over 2,000 known designs. Even when the Gobelins manufactory was beset by financial problems in the late seventeenth century, André-Charles Boulle (1642–1732) – probably the greatest designer in the Louis-Quatorze style – produced furniture for the court from his workshops in the Louvre and collaborated closely with Bérain. His designs for furniture and works in bronze were published in the early eighteenth century.

Once the decorative arts had been established as being of central national interest under Louis XIV, there were very few periods in the next two and a half centuries when this concept was seriously weakened. Perhaps the onslaught of mechanization and industrialization eroded it for a time in the mid and late nineteenth century, but by and large it survived changes of political direction and varieties of government.

In addition to royal and court patronage, other important factors played a part during the eighteenth century to reinforce the maintenance of standards in the applied arts and to ensure that they remained central to the lives of the privileged classes. One of these was the continuing strength of the traditional craft guilds, which encouraged specialization and also the handing down of businesses from father to son, thus building up a reservoir of exceptional skills in the form of dynasties of designers and craftsmen.

The Regency period which followed the death of Louis XIV,

and the reigns of Louis XV and Louis XVI, saw the evolution of design towards more relaxed, informal styles. Smaller, more intimate rooms demanded more delicate artefacts which, by the Louis-Quinze period, had ceased to rely directly on the rectilinear models of classical antiquity. Mirrors and delicate panelling became essential attributes of the new living spaces. The new spirit was very evident in the original sketches of such as Oppenordt (1672–1742), Meissonnier (1693–1750) and Pineau (1684–1754). Oppenordt's designs became widely available after their publication in Paris in 1745. For our knowledge of Meissonnier we are almost completely dependent on a series of 120 published engravings of designs for interiors, furniture and decorative objects in silver and bronze.

Although the skilled designers and craftsmen of Paris and of the great manufactories received a double blow in the Revolutionary period in the suppression of the guilds and the disappearance of their traditional clientèle, with the resultant closure of many *ateliers*, it says much for the strength of the applied arts in France that they re-emerged under the Directoire and Napoleon as central as ever to the nation's self-regard. It was about this time that the engraver Pierre de la Mésangère began the publication of his *Collection de Meubles et Objets de Goût* in the *Journal des Dames et des Modes* which illustrated, notably, the designs of Georges Jacob, whose 'Etruscan' style represented a transitional aesthetic between the Ancien Régime and the Consulate and Empire.

The development of the Jacob company is instructive. After helping to define the decorative repertory of Empire – laurel crowns, helmets, sphinxes, griffons and imperial insignia – it continued dynasty-like to trade until 1847 as Jacob-Desmalter et Cie. Importantly, for the survival of the ideals of excellence in both form and execution, such companies combined the individual craftsmanship of the Ancien Régime with production on a modest industrial scale. The comparison with developments in Great Britain is illuminating; there, massive industrialization had all but swamped any concern for fine design by the mid century. The French under Napoleon, in contrast, trod a delicate line between studio craft and industrial design to create what were, effectively, luxury industries. Napoleon himself, having inherited a number of empty palaces, swiftly began a refurbishment programme under Percier and Fontaine which revitalized a

Sallon.
B.

Salle à Manger

Sallon
Courant

Cheminée du Sallon

number of important craft and manufacturing centres and again underlined the importance of the applied arts to national self-esteem. The porcelain workshops of Sèvres became a Manufacture Impériale; the Savonnerie carpet manufactory (originally founded by Louis XIII in 1627) was revived after 1805; the silk weavers of Lyons received new commissions; and the furniture-makers of Paris who had survived the Revolutionary period now served a burgeoning new market.

The Empire style with which the Jacobs had been so closely associated continued as a distinct design influence through the Restoration period but, befitting a time of increasing middle-class power, overtly imperial features (such as heavy bronze decorations) began to disappear from their designs. The newly wealthy, often living in rented apartments, wanted a style which was elegant but also comfortable. Interiors in general became less grand; wallpaper rather than panelling was used to create a more informal effect. The strictly Napoleonic style of Empire was further eroded by a growing variety and eclecticism in the applied arts: orientalism, medievalism and the styles of the French Renaissance all made their appearance; 'Gothic' appeared in the style known as *troubadour*.

If this eclecticism, which remained prevalent throughout the Second Empire period, seemed for once to indicate a lack of direction in the applied arts in France, there were other positive developments. A number of household names in the luxury goods markets now made their appearance. Christofle, manufacturers of metalware, was founded in 1830; much patronized by Napoleon III for its tableware, the firm also produced furniture and bronze decoration for the revivalist pieces of Second Empire. Hermès followed in 1837, and the jewellers Boucheron in 1858.

This was also a period where the latest fashions in interior design and decoration were widely disseminated in pattern books – some of which are illustrated later in the present work. Pierre de la Mésangère continued to publish his highly influential *Meubles et Objets de goût* in the *Journal des Dames et des Modes* until 1835. The furniture and interior designer M. Santi produced another key publication in 1828: *Modèles de meubles et de décorations intérieures pour l'ameublement*. A furniture designer, Michel Jansen, produced a work specifically directed at other manufacturers in 1835: *Ouvrage sur l'ébénisterie, dédié aux fabricants*. The upholsterer Alphonse Giroux published *Meubles et Fantaisies* in Paris around 1840. A cabinet-maker at the Garde-Meubles Royal, Édouard Lemarchand, issued sets of lithographed designs; the *Cabinet de dessins de fauteuils*. As the century wore on, upholsterers and decorators came more to the fore at the expense of cabinet-makers; in 1836 we find the fashionable interior designer Aimé Chenevard promoting eclecticism in his *Album de l'ornemaniste, recueil d'ornements dans tous les genres et dans tous les styles*. Thirty years later appeared Liénard's *Spécimens de la décoration et de l'ornementation au XIXe siècle*, published in Liège.

Just as the designers and craftsmen of the eighteenth century had been recognized by their European clientèle as pre-eminent in Europe, so a newly wealthy bourgeoisie still looked to France for the fine things of life. During the Second Empire and, later, the Third Republic, the decorative arts remained at the centre of national self-concern, but in an essentially middle-class form. In this Napoleon III and the Empress Eugénie exercised a strong influence, refurbishing their palaces with a middle-class zeal for comfort. The styles of the late seventeenth and early eighteenth centuries were extensively plundered, often with specific effects in mind. Thus, the *salon* of one of the apartments in the buildings along Haussmann's new boulevards might be Louis-Quatorze or Louis-Quinze, while the bedroom would be more likely to be styled in a Louis-Seize mode. Along with the taste for eighteenth-century effects – also promoted in the luxury goods industries by such firms as Baccarat and Christofle – went a taste for opulence. The upholsterer (*tapissier*) began to overshadow the cabinet-maker as more heavily padded furniture appeared. He would also be responsible for coordinating the other elements in room settings, which now veered towards deep reds and greens, with a profusion of draped hangings, combinations which could easily degenerate into vulgar display – *le goût Ritz*. Again, the shift in taste towards the coordinated interior can be found widely evidenced in the pattern books of the time; such publications as A. Simoneton's *La Décoration Intérieure* illustrated complete room settings in a variety of so-called 'national' and 'ethnic' styles.

Much of the production of furniture and of decorative artefacts at this time was of a reasonably high order, high enough at least to maintain France's position as the leading provider of luxury goods. But, while popular taste still pillaged the past, other influences were making themselves felt. As early as 1856 Comte Léon de Laborde had published his *De l'Union des Arts et de l'Industrie*, which advanced Ruskin-like arguments against the abuses of mass-production. In 1877 the Union Centrale des Arts Décoratifs was founded to promote principles of fine original design and sound craftsmanship along lines similar to those proposed by William Morris and his disciples in England. Indeed, the Arts and Crafts Movement was one of the sources of the new ideas which swept through French design in the latter part of the nineteenth century to create the style we know generally as Art Nouveau, most forcefully defined by the great Paris exhibition of 1900. Although the new design style was fresh and innovative, it did look towards traditional French values of fine workmanship and respect for materials. It also looked outside to other cultures for visual inspiration – notably to the Far East. Yet this was also a movement of artists, creating exotic forms for an enlightened clientèle in what were effectively design studios. Gallé, Majorelle and Daum in Nancy, Guimard in Paris brought a new intensity to the debate between art, design and production. And such publications as *Art et Illustration* followed this dialogue with enthusiasm, while the pattern books multiplied.

In many ways the emergence of individual artist-designers, working from their own studios, gave French decorative arts in the early twentieth century the air of having returned to the eighteenth. The new generation accorded the same importance to adventurous design and fine materials as the Rococo masters. This process was to gather even more force among the designers within the style now known universally as Art Deco, where the great *ensembliers* sought to bring the finest skills of French cabinet-making, weaving, pottery-making and glass-blowing to the furnishing of splendid interiors embellished by rare and exotic materials. In no other country were such high standards of design and execution in the decorative arts attained and promoted in the first two decades of the twentieth century. Because the Art Deco style has always been defined to a large extent by the exhibition of 1925, it is sometimes forgotten that it did in fact follow almost directly on Art Nouveau – only the postponement of the Exposition Internationale des Arts Décoratifs et Industriels Modernes because of World War I caused the interi-

ors of Ruhlmann and Süe et Mare, the glass of Lalique and Baccarat, the metalware of Christofle to become firmly identified as *the* definitive style of the twenties rather than of a decade earlier. But whatever the date, Art Deco proper was magnificently French and a powerful restatement of the superiority of French applied arts first so trenchantly declared to the rest of Europe in the reigns of Louis XIV and Louis XV.

At the same time as the masters of Art Deco were reaffirming their traditional and exclusive skills, another movement, drawing on far wider-ranging international influences was making itself felt in France: International Modernism. This was altogether a more architecturally inspired movement and, in its divergence from the sumptuousness of high Art Deco, we can see a growing rift between the architect/designer and the decorator/designer. In some cases, as is evident from a number of the plates reproduced in this book, the two styles influenced each other; by and large, however, the ideals of Le Corbusier, Pierre Chareau and Charlotte Perriand remained at odds with those of the master *ensembliers* of Art Deco. But such was the interest in interior design at the time, both styles were extensively promoted in publications devoted to particular types of artefact and, especially, in reproductions of complete *ensembles*. Designs by the École Martine, the school founded by the *couturier* Paul Poiret, were published in *Décor Moderne*; complete settings by a variety of designers appeared in the *Répertoire du Goût Moderne*, the *Collection Décors et Couleurs* and *Intérieures Français*.

The problem of deciding what to reproduce in this book as representative of the extraordinary flowering of the decorative arts in France during the inter-war years is one which has – happily, in many ways – affected the compilation of all the chapters, from the heyday of Versailles to World War II. But whether the illustrations have been drawn from company archives – sketches demonstrating with immediacy the craftsman's reactions to his material – or from magnificently printed and produced pattern books, the evidence is ineluctable: the French national archive of decoration and design is of an amazing consistency of excellence and, at its high points, of peerless quality.

de tems dor
nement
par

CD 1509

The Influence of
VERSAILLES

THE PALACE OF VERSAILLES, to which the court of Louis XIV moved in 1682, expressed in a peculiarly concentrated way the ideals of brilliance in intellectual and social life, in art and design, to which the king aspired. In every way it set the tone for courtly and aristocratic life throughout Europe. It was the showpiece for the national style, ably promoted by Colbert and given its design characteristics by Le Brun: gilt and stucco, high mirrors, marble panelling, allegorical paintings, *trompe-l'oeil* effects and marvellously crafted furniture. It was indeed an appropriate setting for the most powerful monarch in Europe and a focus for a nation for which the decorative arts and crafts were of supreme importance. Apart from Le Brun, who exercised stylistic control over all manner of furniture and furnishings in his capacity as controller of the Manufacture Royale des Meubles de la Couronne des Gobelins, three key figures help to define the applied arts of the period, both by the artefacts produced under their direction and by the publication of their designs: Jean Le Pautre (1618–82), Jean Bérain (1638–1711) and André-Charles Boulle (1642–1732).

Their design repertory, and that of the Gobelins manufactory, was drawn mainly from classical antiquity crossed, it sometimes seems, with the Baroque of Roman palaces. In addition to the insignia of monarchy used on the furniture specifically destined for Versailles, the iconography of the latter part of the seventeenth century incorporated much imagery drawn from the architecture of ancient Rome: caryatids, terms, pilasters; the plant and animal kingdoms were also plundered – lotus, laurel, oak and acanthus leaves, fruit and various flowers, sea-horses, griffins, horse and goat hooves, lions' heads and paws. In furniture-making the ebony veneers of the period of Louis XIII gave way to veneering with more exotic woods; fine marquetry effects, developed especially by Boulle, were achieved with tortoiseshell, pewter and brass. Furnishing, too, began to display great elaboration towards the end of the century, when rosettes, tasselled fringes and pelmets were steadily introduced.

Of incalculable influence in the dissemination of the Louis-Quatorze style were the engraved designs of Le Pautre which advocated a splendidly monumental approach to design, whether in the detailing of individual pieces or in compositions bringing together furniture and wall design. Typically, his console tables would have legs carved in the form of mythological figures, while classical garlands sweep down from the table top. The table might be shown flanked by two torchères, carved in human form and placed beneath a mirror mounted on a painted wall. The frames of Le Pautre's mirrors were envisaged as substantial sculptures in themselves; side pieces might be formed of hanging garland forms with as many as six putti clinging to them, the whole surmounted by a medallion of a classical bust. His urns, too, though loosely modelled on those of classical antiquity, display a refreshing exuberance in the form of flowers, fruits and foliage among which nymphs and satyrs disport themselves.

If Le Pautre's world was wide and various, a universe of more rather than less, then that of Bérain is distinguished by a lightness and elegance which looked forward to the styles of the Régence or even Louis-Quinze. There is a general light-heartedness in his designs, evident in the use of curved forms, highlighted by dazzling marquetry in brass and tortoiseshell, mother-of-pearl and ivory. The son of a gunsmith from Lorraine, he settled in Paris around 1644, where his first published designs were of decorations for firearms and locks. On Le Brun's death in 1690 he became principal designer to the king, lodging in the Louvre close to his great collaborator, André-Charles Boulle. Although Bérain still drew on a classical vocabulary for the decorative elements of his furniture, panelling and chimney-pieces, often inspired by the grotesques of antiquity which appear in the paintings of Raphaël and Primaticcio, he introduced some of the whimsical imagery which was to be explored more thoroughly in the eighteenth century – figures of Chinamen replacing the gods of classical mythology, monkeys instead of satyrs and fauns. His influence is also discernible in the design of carpets, tapestry and faïence in the early eighteenth century.

Bérain's designs were probably used by André-Charles Boulle for some of the marquetry effects incorporated in his quite distinct furniture which – if anything did – defined the Louis-Quatorze style. Indeed, so powerful were the forms created by him that furniture in his manner continued to be made throughout the eighteenth century and well into the nineteenth, when it enjoyed a resurgence of fashion during the Second Empire. Boulle's original designs were characterized by monumental forms, beautifully coordinated and articulated, and quite magnificent marquetry in tortoiseshell and brass. Because cabinet-makers did not individually stamp their work at the time, very few pieces can be directly attributed to Boulle, although it is known that he made two *commodes* for the king's bedroom at the Grand Trianon and received commissions from the French nobility and foreign royalty, including Philip V of Spain and the Electors of Bavaria and Cologne. Again, it is the published record which permits us to appreciate the full range of Boulle's design talents; in this case, the *Nouveaux Desseins de Meubles et Ouvrages de Bronze et de Menuiserie inventés et gravés par A.-C.*

Boulle, probably published in the early eighteenth century.

Another early eighteenth-century publication was the *Oeuvres* of Daniel Marot, a Huguenot who may have worked in the Boulle workshops before moving to the service of William of Orange, first in the Netherlands and later in England. His was a pleasant enough version of the Louis-Quatorze style which extended to the design of complete settings, including drapes and pelmets, and individual pieces of furniture. Yet another example of the pan-European status of the styles was the publication in Antwerp c. 1680 of designs by Cornelis Golle by Ertinger, engraver to Louis XIV. By such publications and their dissemination throughout Europe was the pre-eminence of French decorative arts established. The eighteenth century was to see the complete realization of that supremacy.

25

Bibliotheque inuentee et grauée par D. N Marot auec preuillege des Etats Generaux des prouinces Vnie et d'hollande et West Frise

Liure d'appartement Inuenté par Marot Architecte du Roy.

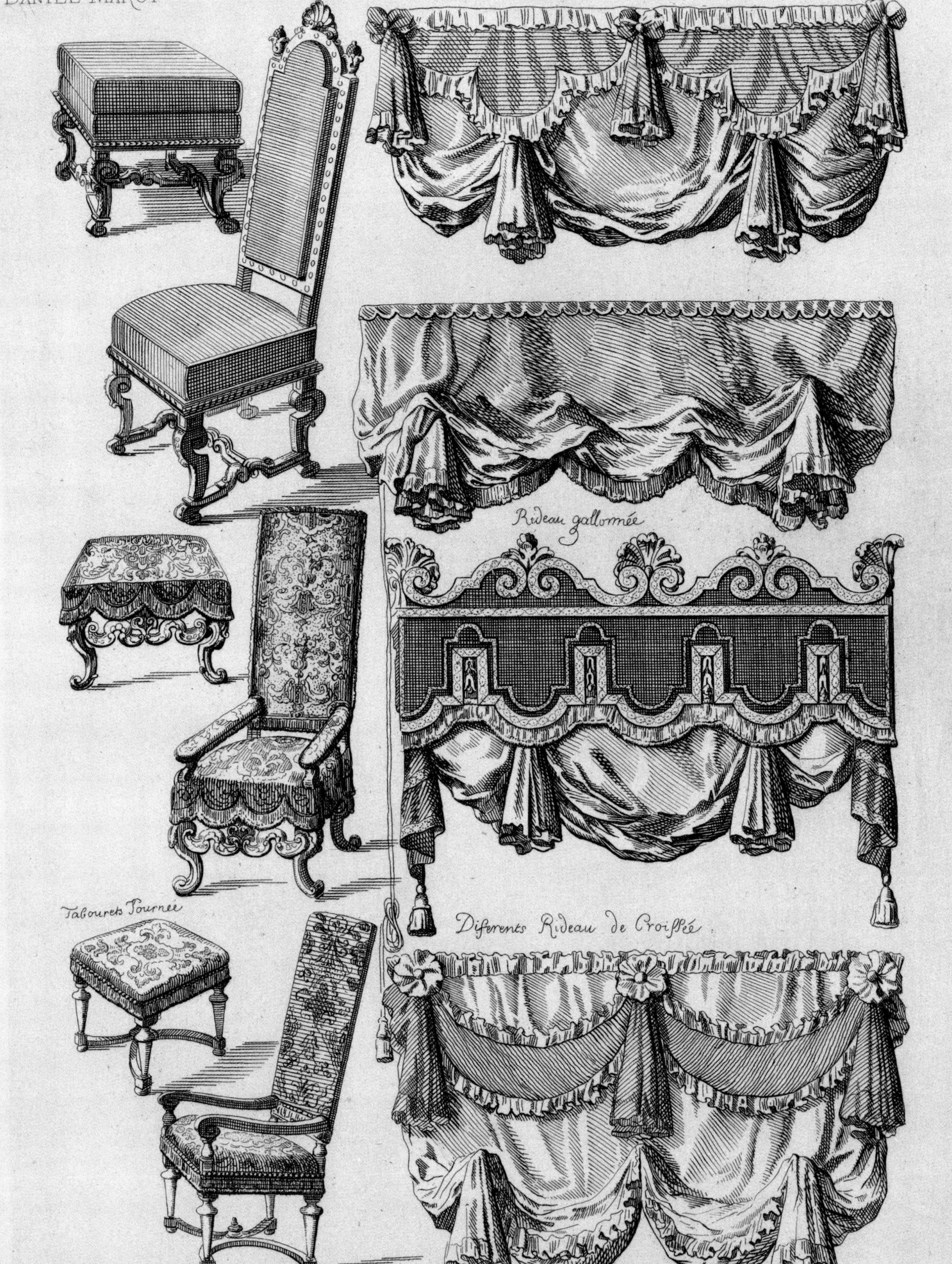
Rideau gallonnée
Tabourets Tournée
Diferents Rideau de Croissée
Marot jn et fecit avec Previlege des Etats generaux et dhollande et Wee frisse.

Paris, RAPILLY, Quai Malaquais, 5.

Imp. Ch. Chardon aîné, Paris

Ecritoire de Cabinet qui porte deux chandeliers

Coffre de toillette monté sur son pied.

Ecritoire

Desseins différens de Bur
veus de face, Et placés à ce

de cabinet

ux de cabinet dans l'aspect qu'ils presentent, etant
de leur Serre-papier.

Armoire qui s'ouvre par les
deux bouts, et sur la quelle est
posé le Serre papier

R. Pfnor sc.

FRANCOIS.I. LOVIS.XII. CHARLES.VIII. LOVIS.X

S.THOMAS ARISTOTE

THOMAS A KEMPIS ERASME

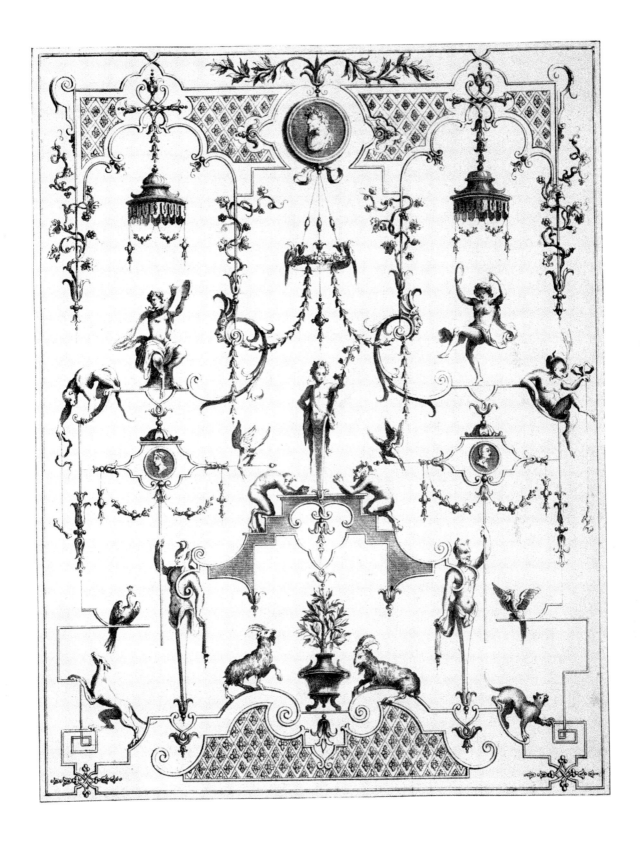

I. Berain, inuenit.   A   M. Daigremont sculpsit.

I. Bersin, jnvenit.   Se vend chez M. Thuret aux Galleries du Louvre C.P.R.   A   M. Daigremont sculpsit.

Jean le Pautre jnv. et fecit.

34

Jean le Pautre inv. et fecit.

39

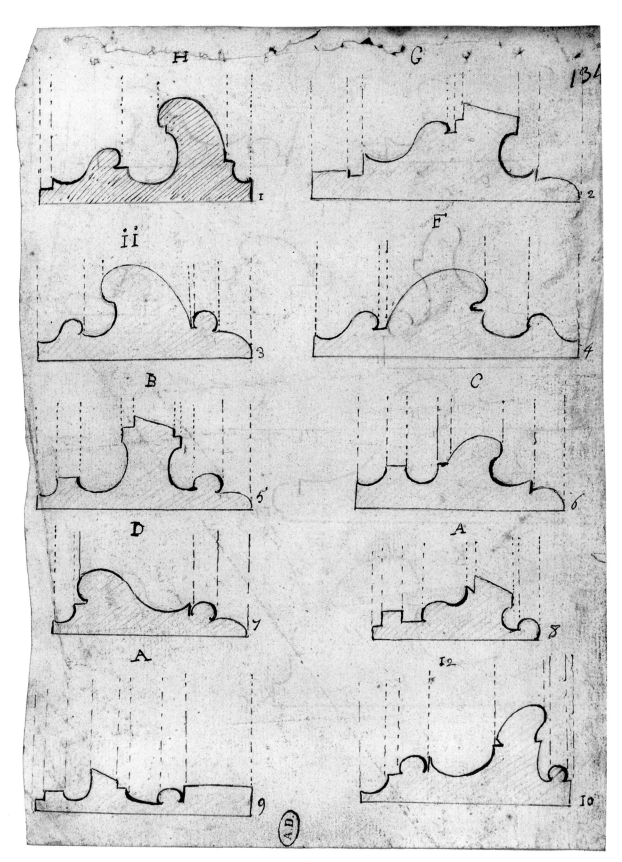

H

G

ii

F

B

C

D

A

A

12

1

2

3

4

5

6

7

8

9

10

A.D.

1

The influence of
VERSAILLES

page 25

Although dating from the last years of the reign of Louis XIV, *c*. 1700–10, these designs for ornamental panels do have a certain lightness and frivolity which points to the more relaxed aspects of the Régence and Louis-Quinze styles.

pages 26–27

One influential publication in the spread of the Louis-Quatorze style through Europe was the *Oeuvres* of Daniel Marot (1663–1752), published in 1702. Marot may very well have worked in the *atelier* of André-Charles Boulle before being forced to flee to the Netherlands because of his Huguenot beliefs. His version of French Baroque extended to complete room-settings as well as designs for individual items, such as chairs, stools and pelmets. The two interiors illustrated here are profoundly and elaborately architectural in

their treatment. Probably designed for William III of the Netherlands, the library (*p. 26 above*) incorporates book-cases whose design, with globes and busts on the upper shelves, seems directly derived from the façades of contemporary buildings. Marot was clearly also an admirer of the upholsterer's art, for which he made many individual designs (*p. 27*) as well as using heavy fabrics to achieve a sumptuous yet unified effect in complete room designs (*p. 26 below*). Note how the wall-hangings in this scheme for a state bedroom are used to continue the forms of the bed drapes. The arrangement of the chairs around the wall is an indication of the deeply-held sense of formality in the European court life of the time.

pages 28–29

The influence of André-Charles Boulle (1642–1732)

was by no means confined to the period of his working life. His furniture designs continued to be reproduced and interpreted by cabinet-makers until well into the nineteenth century. The forms of his furniture and wall-designs, published in the early eighteenth century as *Nouveaux Desseins de Meubles et Ouvrages de Bronze et de Menuiserie*, are characterized by a sumptuousness and opulence which nevertheless always seems to be under the control of the designer-craftsman. The range of his designs was considerable, as these pages show, but perhaps he is best remembered for his monumental *commodes,* tables and cabinets, with their superbly worked gilt-bronze mounts and pedestals, and surfaces rendered fascinating by elaborate marquetry in brass, tortoiseshell and pewter.

page 30

A cabinet of curiosities; one of a series of 1688 engravings by F. Ertinger, engraver to Louis XIV.

pages 31–33

The deft, whimsical touch of Jean Bérain (1638–1711) is abundantly evident in this sheet of decorative designs, now held in the Bibliothèque Forney, Paris. Although he still drew on a traditional vocabulary for his designs and, indeed, became chief designer to Louis XIV, he introduced imagery in human and animal forms which was not totally derived from classical antiquity and looked forward in many ways to the early and mid eighteenth century. His early designs were intended for application to various artefacts, including firearms and locks. His furniture designs (*pp. 32– 33*), some of which were probably used by André-Charles Boulle, are characterized by

1

The influence of VERSAILLES

their exaggeratedly curved forms and called for a dazzling display of the art of marquetry in materials which might include brass, tortoiseshell, mother-of-pearl and ivory. Bérain's designs were eventually published in Paris in the year of his death as *Oeuvres de Jean Bérain, recueillies par le soin du sieur Thuret*, from which these pages are taken.

pages 34–35

The dissemination of the French court style throughout Europe during the latter part of the seventeenth century was due to a number of factors and individuals; one figure, however, does stand out as the design presence of the period – Jean Le Pautre (1618–82). His designs included huge chimney-pieces, complete wall schemes, elaborately carved tables and chairs, free-standing figures and grotesque urns, all

characterized by a heavily Baroque touch. Le Pautre was undoubtedly the most able interpreter of the official Louis-Quatorze style as it had developed under Charles Le Brun at the Gobelins manufactory and at Versailles itself, although the sheer monumentality of his treatments sometimes seems to overwhelm the fundamental forms of his furniture and room-settings. Over two thousand separate engravings of his designs are known to exist. Sold either singly or in sets in Paris, they would have found their way into the workshops of cabinet-makers throughout the French provinces and to the courts of what was considered to constitute civilized Europe.

pages 36–37

The urn was one of the favoured forms of the French Baroque designers. These two splendidly monumental creations were

published in Antwerp by F. Ertinger, engraver to Louis XIV. One of them (*p. 36*) is by Cornelis Golle, a Dutchman who worked in the French manner; his father, Pierre Golle, is mentioned in Louis XIV's account books.

pages 38–39

In contrast to the Baroque extravaganzas of Le Pautre, some of the interiors included in Daniel Marot's books of designs (*see p. 26*) appear almost eighteenth-century in their comparatively restrained use of ornament and in their classical rectilinearity. Many of Marot's designs were intended for the houses of William of Orange, including the palace of Het Loo. When William acceded to the throne of England in 1694, Marot followed him, and examples of his designs can be seen at Hampton Court and Kensington Palace. His room-settings give especial prominence to

the chimney-piece, as in the two examples illustrated here, in which both French and Dutch characteristics are incorporated. He returned to the Netherlands in 1698, where he published two important sets of engravings: *Nouvelles cheminées à panneaux de glace à la manière de France* and the *Nouveau livre de cheminées à la Hollondoise*.

page 40

This page of moulding profiles is taken from an album in the collection of the Musée des Arts Décoratifs, Paris. They are thought to represent forms used in the château of Versailles.

page 43

Looking to the mid century; this project for a *cloche* design shows the imaginative flourishes which characterized French tableware design of the seventeen-fifties.

Ces feuillages sont
ciselés mais point
en bas reliefs

Hauteur et Grandeur des Cloches

Profondeur

Plat quarré

43

The Triumph of
ROCOCO

BY THE BEGINNING of the eighteenth century the taste for Baroque grandeur associated with the reign of Louis XIV had in fact already begun to wane. Even Versailles, that showpiece of the previous century, became less central to the development of the decorative arts as the aristocracy increasingly moved their main residences to Paris to seek a more relaxed life-style away from the pomp of the court. This new mood had very obvious effects on design and decoration and was much encouraged by Philippe d'Orléans during his eight years as Regent for the young Louis XV. During the period of the Régence forms and colours became noticeably less heavy, reflecting the relaxing of the claustrophobic atmosphere of the court in the last years of Louis XIV's reign and a new-found enthusiasm for entertainment. Focus shifted from large state rooms to the more intimate settings of *salon* and boudoir, demanding smaller, lighter furniture with more obviously graceful lines. The taste for the delicate effects of *chinoiserie* was another reflection of the new and fashionable informality.

The Regent himself was instrumental in promoting the new styles, notably by two significant personal appointments: Gilles-Marie Oppenordt (1672–1742) as official Architect and Director-General of Buildings and Gardens, and Charles Cressent (1685–1758) as the court *ébéniste*, following the death of Jean Poitou. Cressent had begun his working life as a sculptor in Amiens, moving later to Paris, where he married Poitou's widow and took over the workshop of the dead *ébéniste*. His known designs are indeed sculptural in their introduction of opulent curves and figurative mounts which point towards fully-fledged Rococo. Unfortunately for attribution, *ébénistes* were not obliged at that time to stamp their work personally; however, enough pieces exist which have been ascribed to him with certainty to mark him as one of the most influential designers of the early eighteenth century. There is no such problem, however, in assessing Oppenordt's influence, since he was a prolific draughtsman, turning his hand to designing a variety of artefacts and decorations, both interior and exterior. Beginning in a distinctly Baroque style, he gradually developed a proto-Rococo manner, notable especially in designs for complete room-settings and chimney-pieces. Although his version of Rococo fell far short of the curvilinear extravagances of Meissonnier and Pineau, his influence was nevertheless extensive, largely because of the posthumous publication by Jacques-Gabriel Hugier, an engraver and ornamental designer, of three collections of Oppenordt's works, containing designs for virtually every artefact known to interior decoration: mouldings, cartouches, panels, chandeliers and splendid chimney-pieces.

The innovations of these designers were accepted with alacrity by the court patrons of the age. For the first time within the post-Renaissance era, the decorative arts freed themselves from classical references and declared for voluptuous, sensuous forms which were to captivate France and the rest of Europe for the next thirty years, before yielding again to the more insistent claims of classicism. Indeed, the Louis-Quinze style in its purest form was actually quite short-lived: it had not developed fully during the regency of Philippe d'Orléans, who died in 1723, yet it had already declined in the face of Neoclassicism by the time of Louis XV's death in 1774.

This was a period of rampant individualism in the decorative arts; one senses in the convoluted scrolling effects of much of high Rococo and in its wilful denial of rectilinearity the aspiration of designer and craftsman to the status of artist. It was at this time – in 1743 – that the statutes of the main guilds were revised, notably those of the Corporation des Menuisiers-Ébénistes, to require all master craftsmen to stamp their work individually. Although this measure was ostensibly taken to undermine the position of the so-called 'free' craftsmen who operated outside the guilds, it does seem to reflect a certain affirmation of the creative status of the designer-craftsman. And, certainly, the two pre-eminent figures of high Rococo – the *genre pittoresque* – could be so described, since their influence was spread more by the publication of their designs than by any finished artefact or completed interior design. These were Juste-Aurèle Meissonnier (1695–1750) and Nicolas Pineau (1684–1754).

The son of a Provençal goldsmith and sculptor working in Turin, Meissonnier moved to Paris in 1720; there, he rapidly established himself as an interior designer, silversmith and architect, becoming the official Architecte-dessinateur de la Chambre et du Cabinet du Roi. However, in spite of his eminence, very few works directly attributable to him survive; we depend largely on the publication of some one hundred and twenty published engravings for an evaluation of his work. These show a predilection for voluptuously curvilinear forms, applied especially to artefacts in metal, such as candelabra. Important, too, are his designs for complete interiors, often focused on an imaginative elaboration of the chimney-piece. These designs undoubtedly inspired a generation of cabinet-makers and craftsmen; their asymmetrical curves and scrolls can be recognized in the design vocabulary of the prominent *ébénistes* of the time:

Mathieu Criaerd, Jacques Dubois and Bernard van Risen Burgh.

The lines of Pineau's work were less violently exciting in their denial of rectilinearity than Meissonnier's. But, like the latter's, they were dependent for their influence on publication rather than incarnation as finished pieces. His distinctive repertory of shells, flowers and palms ornamenting curving surfaces was often imitated, thanks to a series of engravings by Mariette. Though born in Paris, Pineau first came to notice as an interior designer in Russia, where he created panelling at Peterhof for Peter the Great. Eventually he returned to Paris, where he rapidly established himself as one of the most fashionable designers of the time, capable of calling on the finest cabinet-makers, such as Cressent, for the execution of his stylish creations. Everywhere there is a sense of movement, almost liquid, in the smooth curves of the designs, reflecting perhaps the derivation of some motifs of Rococo – *le style rocaille* – from the grottoes fashionable at the time: rocks, shells and waterfalls. But not all designers embraced the revolutionary new forms; others, like Pierre Migeon, who took over the family business from his similarly named father in 1739, continued to work in the simpler styles of the Régence. For such workshops which worked conservatively within the confines of the Louis-Quatorze and Régence style, the swing of taste to Neoclassicism in the seventeen-fifties and seventeen-sixties represented relatively little in the way of change.

pages 46–47, 52 and 54
It is a remarkable testimony to the brilliance of Juste-Aurèle Meissonnier (1695–1750) that his towering reputation as a master of Rococo rests largely on a relatively small number of designs published between 1723 and 1735. His style is characterized by elaborate, asymmetrical scroll-work which he applied equally to wall-panelling and to free-standing objects, including candlesticks (*p. 54*), tables and chairs. This project for a doorway (*p. 52*) dates from *c.* 1733.

page 48
Another page from Diderot's great *Encyclopédie*; this plate shows cutlery-makers at work.

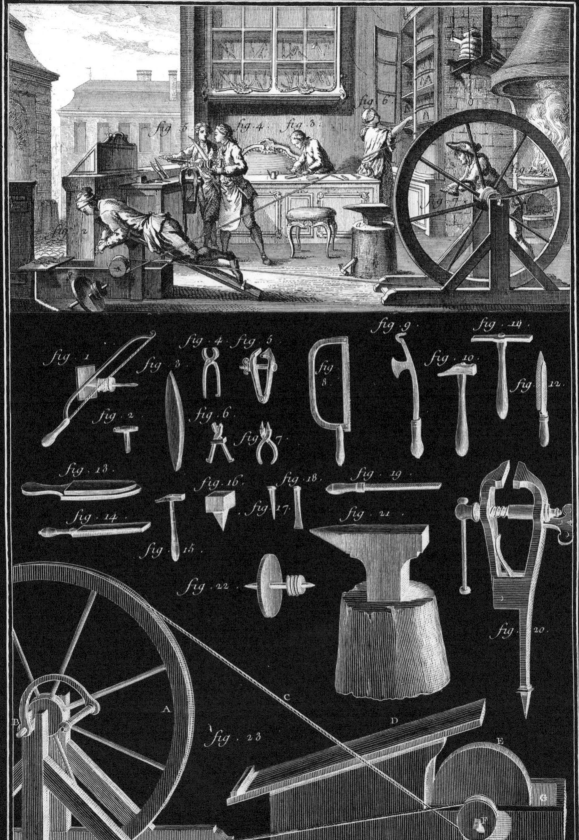

Pl. I.

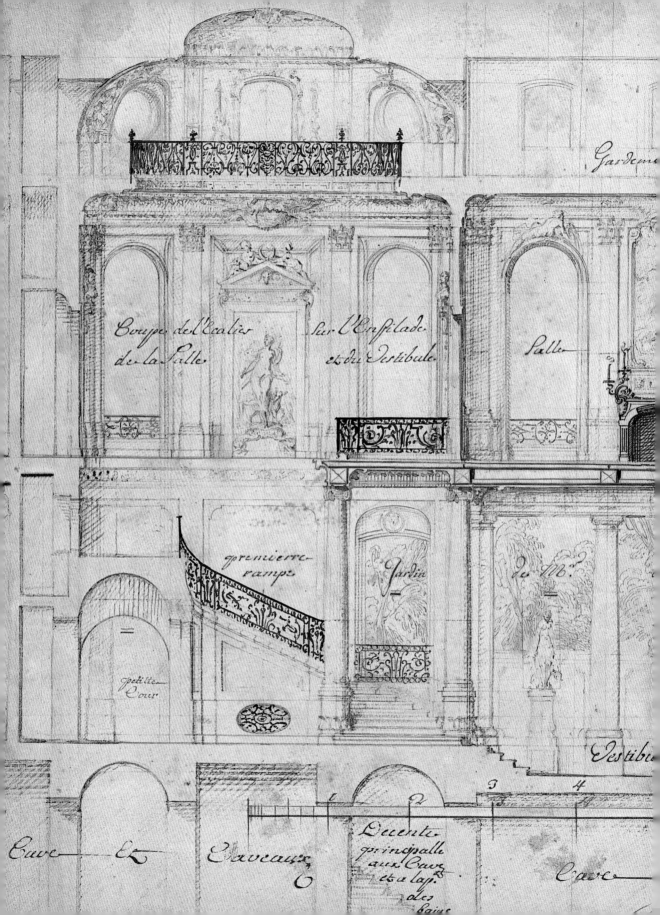

Gardens

Coupe de l'Escalier   Sur l'Enfilade   Salle
de la Salle   et du Vestibule

premiere
rampe   Jardin   de M.

petitte
Cour

Vestibule

Cave   Et   Caveaux   Descente   Cave
principalle
aux Caves
et a la
des
bains

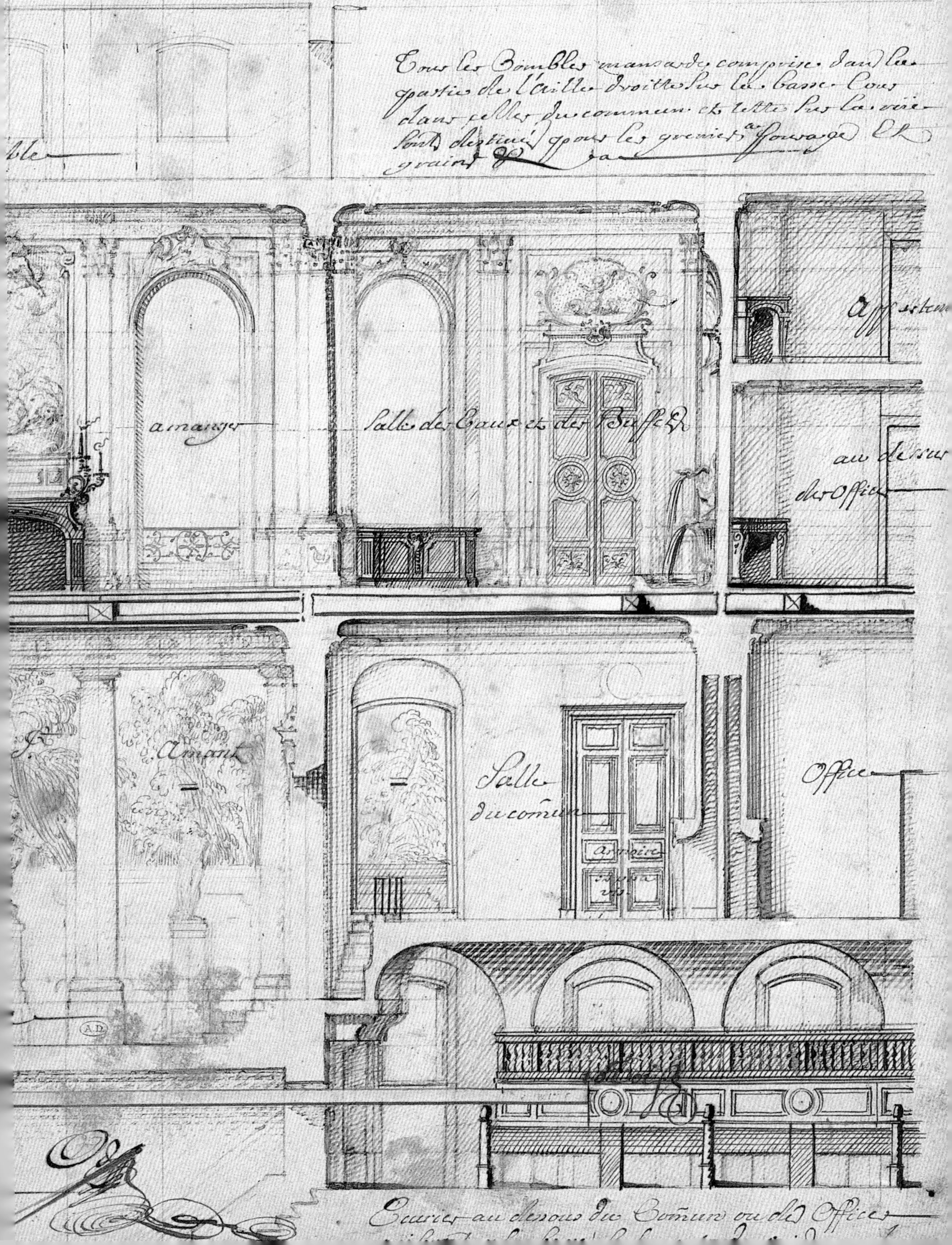

Tous les Combles mansardes comprise dans la
partie de l'aille droitte sur la basse-Cour
dans celles du commun et tette sur la voie
sont destiné pour les greniers à fourrage et
grains

a manger

Salle de Caur et des Buffet

Appartement

au dessus
des Office

Amour

Salle
du commun

Armoire

Office

Cuisier au desous du Commun ou des Offices

83

J.O. Meissonnier in.

Aquier Sculp et ex. C.P.R. a Paris rue St Jacques

Cabinet de M.^r le Comte Bielinski Grand Marechal de la Couronne de Pologne executé en 1734.

A Paris chés Huquier rue St Jacque au coin de celle des Mathurins CPR.

Oppenord inv.   *Huquier ex. rue S. Jacques C.P.R.*

LIVRE DE CHEMINÉE ET LAMBRIS DE MENUISERIE ET DE SCULPTURE PAR G.M. OPPENORD ARCHITECTE.

Paris chez Huquier rue des Mathurins au coin de celle de Sorbonne. C.P.R.

Cheminées et Lambris pour un Sallon à l'Italienne.   Huquier Sculp. et ex. rue des Mathurins C.P.R.

60

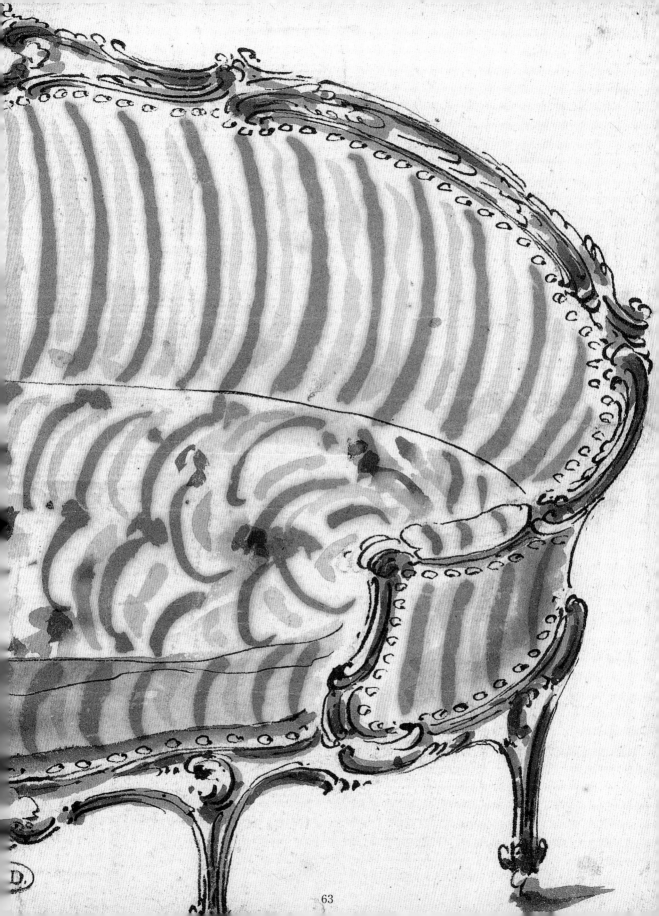

63

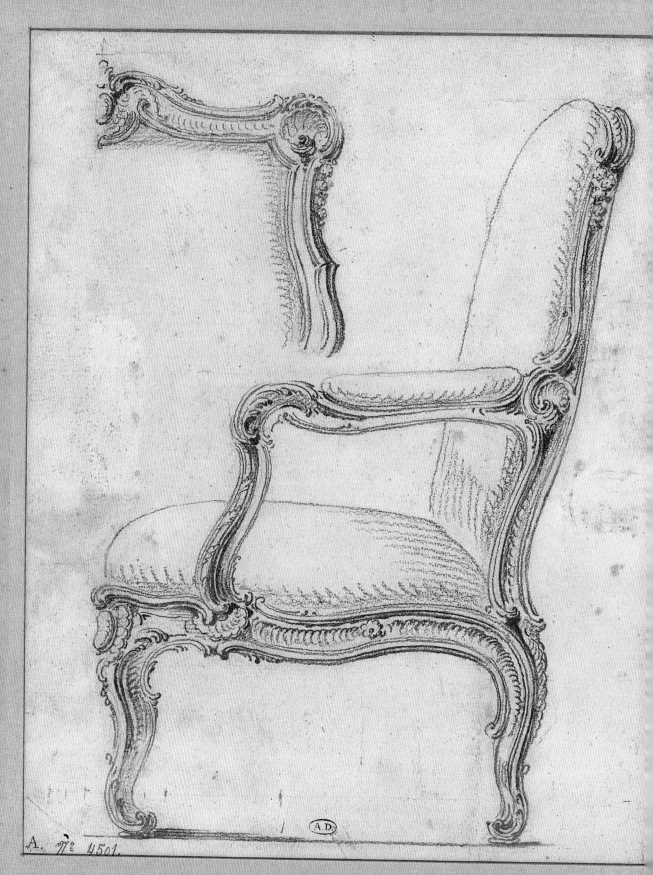

A. N° 4501.

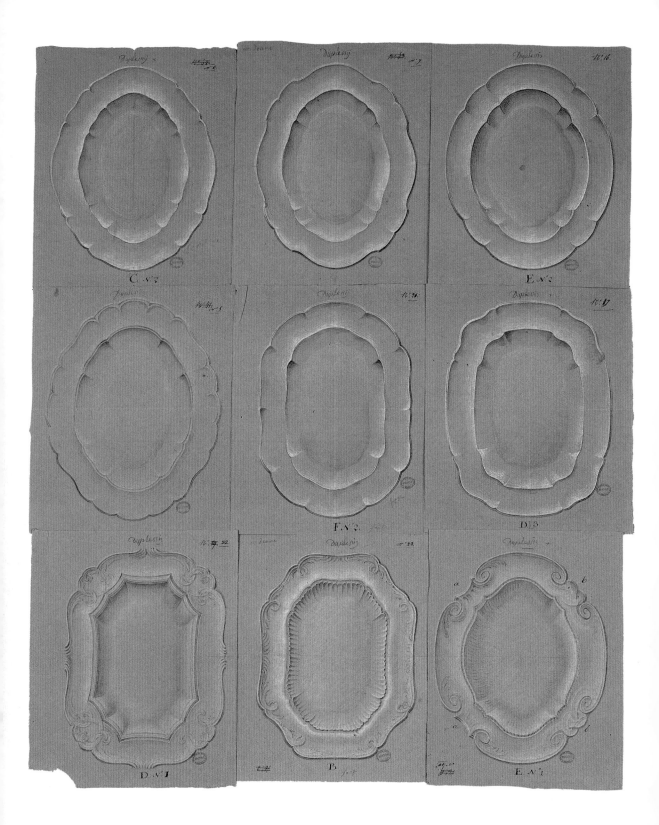

71

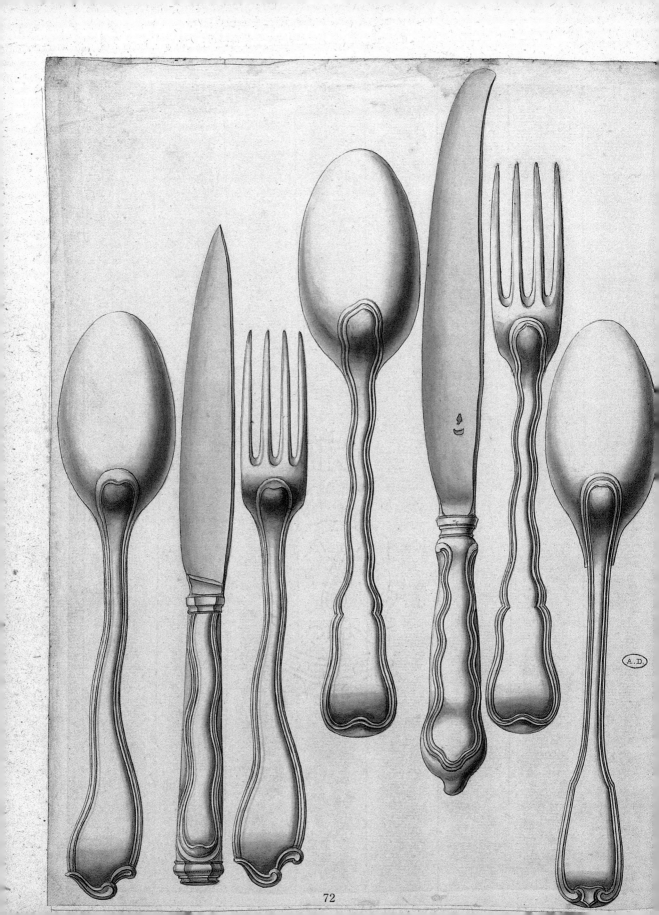

73

A.D

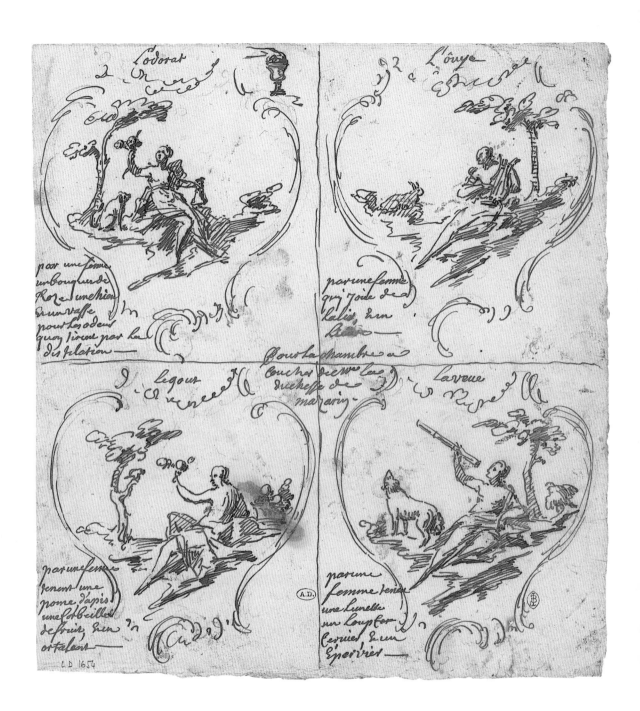

L'odorat

par une femme
un bouquet de
Rose une chien
en un vase
pour les odeurs
quy fiont par la
distillation —

L'ôüye

par une femme
quy joüe de
Kalis, en un
lieu —

pour la chambre a
Coucher de Mre les
duchesse de
mazarin —

le gout

par une femme
tenant une
pomme d'apis
une Corbeille
de fruit, en un
ortaleux —

La veue

par une
femme tenen
une Lunette
un Loupter
Cervier, en un
Epervier —

A.D.

LD 1654

H. Gravelot inv.

D. N° 368 bis

377

A.D.

troisième rampe

Segonde rampe

premiere rampe

2

The triumph of
ROCOCO

2
The triumph of
ROCOCO

2

The triumph of
ROCOCO

while those on the right-hand page seem already to be tending towards the cleaner, straighter lines which characterized the Neoclassicism of the latter part of the century.

pages 74–75

These two plans for table-settings, dating from the mid eighteenth century, may conceivably have been drawn up for use at the court of Versailles. This display, with its massive deployment of silverware and other fine table ornament, was exactly the kind of showpiece which stamped the authority of French domestic design on all the courts and great houses of Europe during the eighteenth century.

pages 76–77

These exquisite designs in ink and grey wash for two *cloches* and for a plate with *cloche* could very well have been the origin of some of the silverware which embellished the table settings illustrated on *pp. 74–75*. There is a delicious, flowing, sculptural quality in the elaboration of the crowning pieces, an inventiveness allied to the highest standards of execution which were the hallmarks of the decorative arts in eighteenth-century France.

pages 78–79

The human figure, often in graceful and relaxed poses, exercised a peculiar fascination for the designers of mid eighteenth-century France. Elegantly seductive are the sinuous lines of Nicolas Pineau in these four figurative designs (*p. 78*) in pen and brown ink for panels intended for the bedroom of the Duchesse de Mazarin. Roughly contemporary to Pineau was the painter, designer and engraver Hubert-François Gravelot (1699–1773); his designs (*p. 79*) are characterized by their finesse of execution and their acute attention to detail. Best-known for his book illustrations, Gravelot also had a distinguished career as an engraver in London before definitively settling in Paris in 1754.

page 80

Again, the elegant invention of Nicolas Pineau is sublimely translated in these red-chalk sketches for staircase banisters. Roughly dated 1754, the year of Pineau's death, one can perhaps already detect a lessening of the sheer exuberance which had marked the design of the high period of Rococo. These designs were also intended for the Paris house of the Duchesse de Mazarin.

The New CLASSICISM

The reaction to Rococo came relatively early in France, although the style lingered in other parts of Europe – another testament to the widely perceived supremacy of French design. By 1754, Nicolas Cochin, an engraver, was already arguing for a return to the classical ideals of the previous century in his *Supplication aux Orfèvres, Ciseleurs et Sculpteurs sur bois*. This rapid shift in taste during the seventeen-fifties and sixties was partly though not entirely due to renewed interest in classical antiquity and, more specifically, the art and architecture of ancient Greece and Rome. Significantly, Cochin was asked to accompany the future Marquis de Marigny, brother of Madame de Pompadour, on a tour of Italy between 1749 and 1751, as the sibling of the royal mistress prepared to become Directeur-Général des Bâtiments. And, indeed, some of the most significant orders for furniture in the new style came from those most intimately related to the king. Both Madame de Pompadour and Madame du Barry were partial to the newly revived classical style.

Like most changes in taste, the sudden growth in popularity of Neoclassicism is hard to fathom, but the reaction against the curvilinear frivolity of Rococo did happen quickly. By the time of Louis XVI's accession to the throne in 1774 the style was already fully developed. Was it a reflection of a deeply felt need for order and stability before the revolutionary storm of the late 1780s, or does every fashion tend to produce, as its successor, a taste for contrasting forms? Whatever the explanation, the exuberant flourishes and curves of the mid-century gave way to lines derived directly from Greek and Roman models.

A key figure in the transition from Louis-Quinze to Louis-Seize was Jean-François Oeben (*c.* 1721–63). German by birth, Oeben came to Paris between 1741 and 1749, serving initially an apprenticeship in the Boulle family workshops. Later, he opened his own business and was master to the most eminent *ébéniste* of the Louis XVI era, Jean-Henri Riesener (1734–1806). His work is characterized by a very noticeable modifying of the exaggerated curves of Rococo; his marquetry, too, is marked by a more geometrical approach, either in the form of cubes, lozenges and rosettes or floral forms.

The new styles were amply recorded in published records. Jacob Roubo (1739–91), a furniture-maker and designer, published his influential *Art du Menuisier* between 1769 and 1775, which included both Rococo and Neoclassical designs. The garlands and swags so characteristic of the latter were incorporated more emphatically in the engraved designs of Jean-Charles Delafosse (1734–91), which he started to publish just as the interest in classical iconography was beginning to make itself apparent in the developing Louis-Seize style. Delafosse's interests were diverse, to judge from the multiplicity of artefacts for which he produced designs: vases, trophies, cartouches, metalwork, as well as furniture. These were published from 1768 onwards as the *Nouvelle Iconologie Historique*, running through several editions until 1785. Antique ornamentation, including trophies, leaves and Vitruvian scrolls were also very much the visual vocabulary of Jean-François Forty (*fl.* 1772–90), designer, engraver and metal-worker. Apart from designing ironwork for the École Militaire and the entrance court of the Palais Royal, he published an impressive number of designs for all kinds of furniture, complete interiors, and various types of object. Most notable were his eight-part *Oeuvres de sculpture en bronze contenant Girandoles, Flambeaux, Feux de Cheminées, Pendules, Bras, Cartels, Baromètres…*, and his major work of ecclesiastical design, the monumental three-part *Oeuvres d'orfèvrerie à l'usage des églises*.

It fell, however, to the finest cabinet-maker of the late eighteenth century, Jean-Henri Riesener, to define the fully-fledged Louis-Seize style. Although his early furniture retains a certain curvilinearity – a reflection, no doubt, of his years of apprenticeship in Oeben's workshop – his later work embraced the rectangular forms and straight lines of a powerful Neoclassicism. After 1780, by which time he was designing furniture for Marie-Antoinette, he began to use veneers of satinwood, kingwood and, especially, mahogany, decorated with floral forms in gilt bronze. Some of these pieces are of extreme simplicity and elegance, confining decoration to fluting and such additional effects as foliate drawer handles set in large escutcheons.

None of the other major *ébénistes* of the time achieved quite the standing of Riesener. Notable among them was Jean-François Leleu (1729–1807), who had also been a pupil in the Oeben workshop, and made extensive use of marquetry in his mature work. Though lacking the originality of Riesener, his designs were impressively monumental and an entirely satisfactory expression of the Louis-Seize style. Like others of his generation, he also designed furniture embellished with plaques of Sèvres porcelain.

The latter part of the eighteenth century was too troubled to favour the harmonious development of the Louis-Seize style. It was not that the craft-based workshops completely disappeared, but life for the craftsmen clearly underwent radical change. Firstly, their traditional market, the aristocracy, disappeared; then, in 1791, the craft guilds were suppressed. Under the Direc-

toire, the only stable government of the period (which gave its name to the style of the 1790s), simplification was the order of the day, reflecting the revolutionary ideals of the nation and problems in obtaining some of the exotic materials on which the elaborate craftsmanship of the preceding decades had partly depended. Types of furniture were fewer, although some of the pre-Revolution craftsmen still managed to survive. The workshops of Georges Jacob, for instance, still turned out an extensive range of finely made furniture, though now the heavier Neoclassicism of the Louis XVI era was simplified into a fashion which became known as 'Etruscan'. This style was much promoted by Pierre de la Mésangère in the *Journal des Dames et des Modes*. Chairs with scrolled backs and *sabre* legs appear; the columns which embellished the heavier pieces of the previous decade were now often replaced by pilasters; mahogany veneer was mounted with brass rather than bronze.

Yet the luxury workshops and manufactories of France were soon again to find new vigour, inspired by central patronage. Under the Consulate and Empire the decorative arts were once again seen as a central expression of national prestige. And a number of firms, like that of the Jacobs, continued successfully into the new era, thus providing a link between the Ancien Régime and Imperial France.

---

pages 86-87
The interior of an upholsterer's shop in the seventeen-sixties; the style of the furniture indicates that the original drawing for the engraving was made before full Neoclassicism had taken hold.

page 88
An engraving by N. de Launay, engraver to the kings of France and Denmark; it shows a delightful scene of a decorator making a presentation of wallpaper to a party grouped within a high Louis-Seize interior.

page 89
Jean-Démosthène Dugourc's contribution to the development of the Louis- Seize and Restoration styles was a distinguished one (*see pp. 12–13*). These seven designs in blacklead and watercolour were probably intended for use in silk or tapestry production; they are drawn on separate pieces of paper mounted on a single supporting sheet. Their exact date is not known, but they resemble other works by Dugourc dated between 1782 and 1799.

Idées de Ceintures.

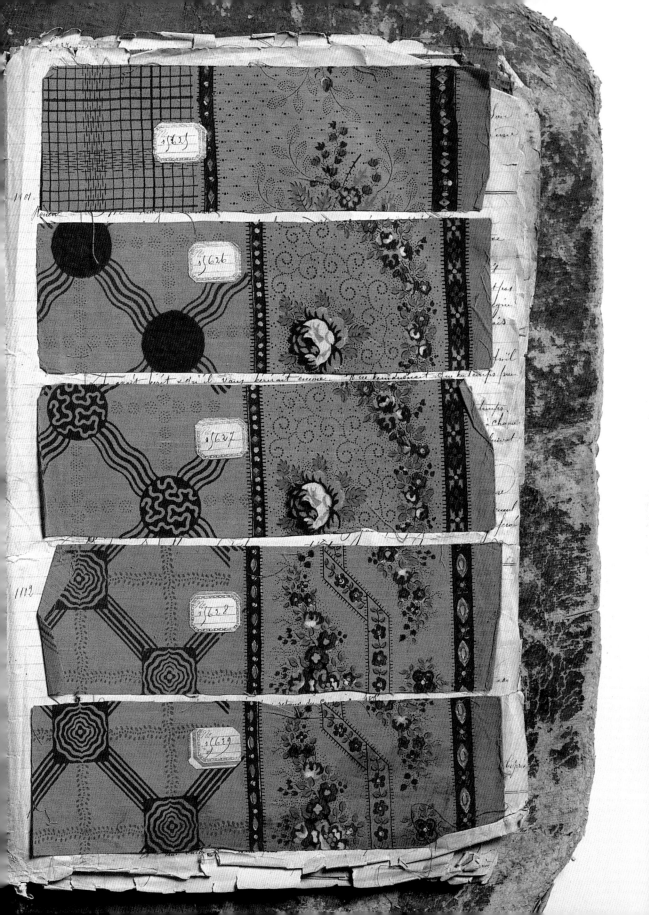

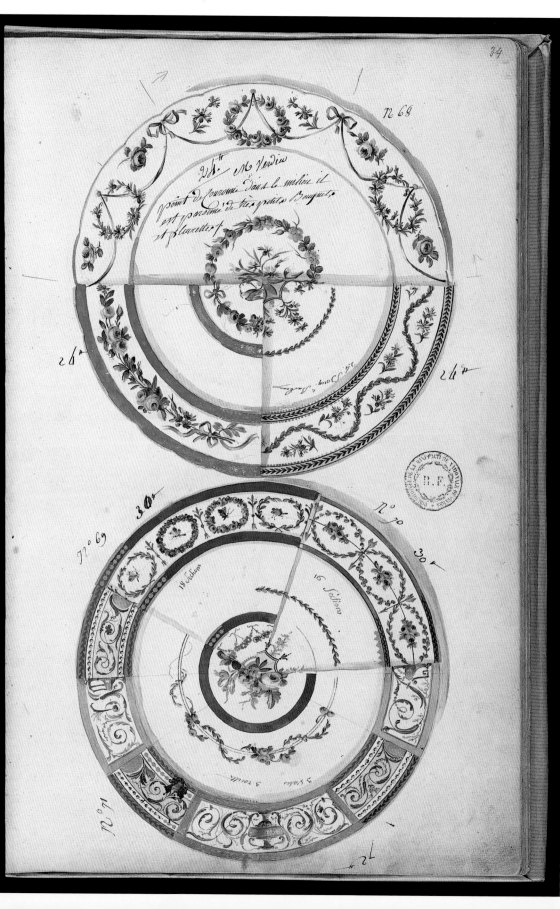

No 68

Mr Verdier
point de Couronne dans le milieu il
est garanie de très petits Bouquets
et fleurettes

26"

26"

26"

30"

No 70

30

No 69

18 Sections

16 Sections

No 71

72"

51

154

153

152

Fourrier brulés
29 Lumiaire an 4
30ᵗ

Milieu de l'assiette du
service du Luxe

156

Restauré à la
peinture en
Pluviose an 6a
24ᵗ

Premier recueil
24 Lumiaire an 4
24ᵗ

Ambassadeur
d'Orient
Pluviose
an 4
155

Ambassadeur d'Espagne ordonné par le
Comité du Gouvernement
157

Série d'Entrée pour Restituer ce qui
y appartient, mais au lieu d'une
bouquet de camaïeu et d'une
jonquille, on met d'une fleur
unie et puis d'un ruban
rose d'effets violet
coloré et nuançé

90ᵗ
La Série a été
faite celui à
bouquets de fleurs
celle de Minerve ou
d'Intérieur et nous
a le faire comme
le petit ou nature dans

158

Ministre du Sénat qui grave
de Pierre Cassel, ordonné
y ... le Gouvernement

27ᵗ

Section D. S. 4. No. 2 — année 1788   No. 28.

Section D. S. 4. année 1788. No. 2.   No. 11.

Exécuté par Xicot. 1775.

Section D. S. 4. année 1788. No. 2.   No. 10.

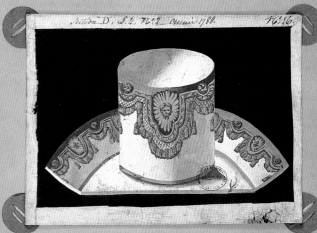

Section D. S. 4. No. 2. année 1788   No. 26.

Section D. S. 4. No. 2. année 1788.   No. 21.

bas.

Section D. S. 4. année 1788. No. 2.   No. 9.

335

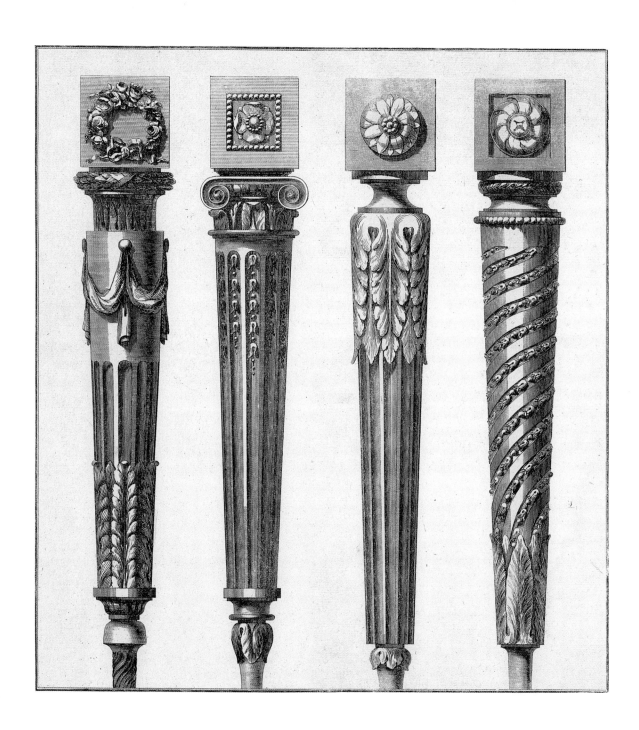

104

Nr 9. D

Durch H. Kruckeufelner gestochen,
cheyolindorst 5ten Juli 1797

N.º 625.

gi a la fabrique

Die Farben der Zeichnung so abfolies wie wir, tc.

109

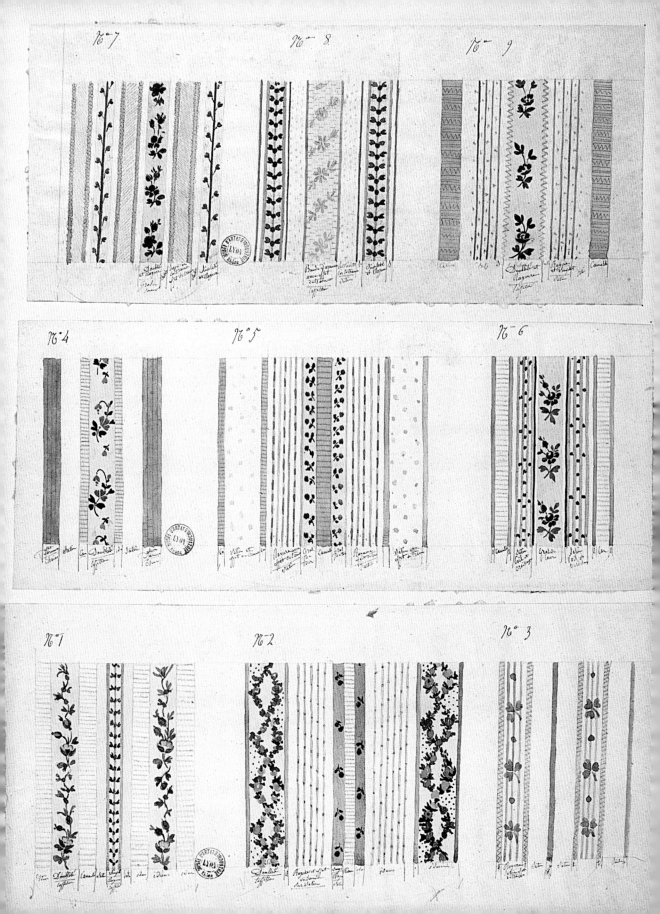

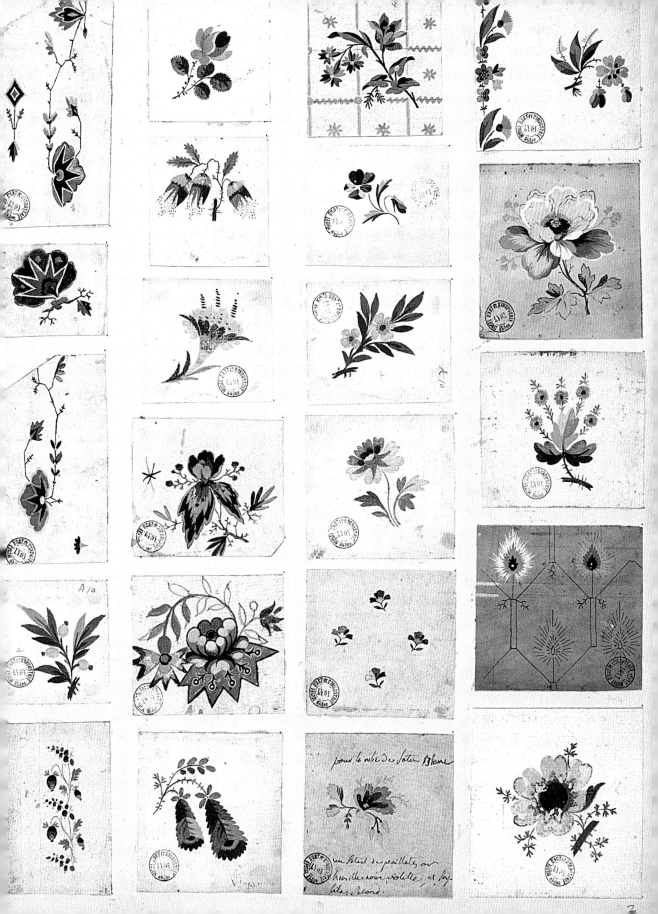

pour la robe de Satin Blanc

un billet de paillette or
feuilles vert violette, et fleurs
lilas blond.

3

The new CLASSICISM

pages 90–91

The production of block-printed cotton fabric in Provence can be traced back to the mid seventeenth century, when workshops were established in Marseilles and in Avignon, in response to the popular demand for coloured cloths first from India and then the Levant. By the mid eighteenth century the French producers had mastered the dyeing techniques used in the Indian workshops and were now capable of producing superb printed cottons, often reflecting in their choice of motifs the local flora and warm colours of the Provençal landscape. · Flowers, herbs and vines were especially popular, giving rise to the term *bonnes herbes* to describe the fabrics. The fabric swatches illustrated here date from 1790 and are among the oldest in the Musée Charles Deméry in Tarascon. The museum was founded in 1938, at the same time that Charles Deméry took over a traditional Tarascon fabric workshop to create the modern company of Souleiado, an old Provençal word which means 'the sun's rays shining through a cloud after the sun', an apt description of these striking colour combinations.

pages 92–93

Textile printing in Mulhouse began about a century later than in the Provençal centres of Marseilles and Avignon (*see pp. 90–91*). Like the dyers of Provence, however, those of Mulhouse drew much of their palette from the colours made popular by imports from the Orient and the Levant. Prominent among the workshops of Mulhouse was Nicolas Koechlin et Frères who developed techniques of printing on linen which had already been dyed to a colour known as *rouge turc*. These swatches are drawn from their archives and are now lodged in the collection of the Musée de l'Impression sur Étoffes, Mulhouse.

pages 94–97

These designs in the archives of the Sèvres porcelain factory date from the years immediately preceding the Revolution. Indeed, the mark used by the factory after 1793 was 'R.F.' (République Française). The production of the period generally reflects the Neoclassical lines of the Louis-Seize style, though decoration remained fairly traditional, drawing on a repertory of largely floral design. Occasionally, though, the immediate stylistic concerns of the time were addressed more directly as, for instance, in this design for cups and borders (*p. 96 below right*).

pages 98–99

This mid eighteenth-century painted panel of an imaginary Chinese emporium highlights the fascination which all things Chinese held for the designers of the eighteenth century. Indeed, by the beginning of the century the importing of Chinese wares, especially porcelain, was already well-established and eventually also influenced the design vocabulary of leading furniture-makers and potters. Figures of dragons and robed Chinamen were turned out by the porcelain manufacturers and even appeared in the supports and mounts of furniture and the frames of looking-glasses. The taste for *chinoiserie* began to decline as the Neoclassical styles of the latter part of the century asserted themselves, although some of its design repertory could still be discerned in textiles, furniture and porcelain until well into the nineteenth century.

3

The new CLASSICISM

Until the seventeen-fifties it had been illegal to produce printed cotton in France, in order to protect the national silk industry. When the embargo against its production was lifted, the relatively new technique of printing on cotton with engraved copper plates was quickly introduced. In 1760 Christophe-Philippe Oberkampf (1738–1815) set up a workshop at Jouy-en-Josas and started production of the famous *toiles de Jouy*, using the plate-printing process on the finest Indian cotton, imported via England. The Jouy workshop became a Manufacture Royale in 1783, at the same time as Jean-Baptiste Huet (1745–1811) was appointed chief designer. Popular with the courtiers of Versailles, designs often showed figures in rustic settings or drew their motifs from the flora and fauna of the natural world or even, as here (*p.*

100), from the *chinoiserie*-inspired designs of Jean-Baptiste Pillement. Designs were usually printed monochrome – indigo, purple, sepia or red – on a white ground. The design on *p. 101* dates from *c.* 1780 and was intended for use at the Nantes Manufacture de Petitpierce Frères.

The design ingenuity and vigour of the Mulhouse textile industry at the end of the eighteenth century are amply demonstrated by these two swatch-book leaves. Each design is a meticulously painted gem on paper, separately mounted in an album now in the Musée de l'Impression sur Étoffes, Mulhouse.

Published in about 1780, the *Cahiers d'Ameublement* by Richard de Lalonde (*fl.* 1780–90) was one of the seminal works of the Louis-Seize style. Intended very

much as a practical manual for the cabinet-maker, it contained a massive selection of designs for every type of furniture and other room furnishings. Although de Lalonde was a thoroughgoing classicist and in the forefront of the reaction against Rococo curves and frivolity, these designs for chair legs do show a concern with variety and ornament, albeit within the rectilinearity of the style.

Closely associated with the cabinet-maker Georges Jacob, the so-called 'Etruscan' style was a fairly short-lived fad which briefly connected the design of the Ancien Régime with that of the Consulate and Empire. Decorative motifs were derived from antiquity – in fact, usually Greek rather than Etruscan – while furniture forms took Neoclassicism another step towards the full-blown Empire style. Chairs, as in

this pencil and ink design of the seventeen-nineties, were notable for curved or scroll backs and back legs *en sabre*.

More examples of the textile designs of the house of Nicolas Koechlin (*see pp. 92–93*); as well as bold abstract design, some of the highly stylized figurative motifs appear to have been derived from the characters of the Commedia dell'Arte.

These two textile designs date from 1797 and are the work of the factory established in Colmar in the latter part of the eighteenth century by Jean-Michel Haussmann (1749–1817). Born in Colmar, Haussmann proved himself an exceptionally gifted chemist, especially in the application of dyes. His first successful business was established in Rouen, where he produced the fashionable textiles

3

The new
CLASSICISM

known, logically, as *rouenneries*. He later returned to Colmar where, after problems with the local water which lacked the alkaline properties of that of Rouen, he established another successful business. His experiments of the period, including his analysis of the role of local waters in dyeing, were of paramount importance in establishing the pre-eminence of the French textile industry by the end of the eighteenth century.

pages 110–111

These delicate floral patterns on pages from swatch-books held by the Musée des Tissus, Lyons, probably served as models for the embroidery of the lighter garments which were coming into fashion during the reign of Louis XVI. By 1778 there were approximately 6,000 female embroiderers in Lyons alone. One garment which lent itself particularly well to the new fashion was the waistcoat (*gilet*), the craze for which was partly due to an interest in all things English.

page 112

During the stewardship of Alexandre Brongniart (1770–1847), the Sèvres porcelain factory enjoyed something of a renaissance, a turn in fortune eventually to be confirmed by the extensive patronage conferred upon it by Napoleon in the early years of Empire. Under Brongniart, appointed in 1800, Sèvres began to adopt a design vocabulary based very much on the more grandiose and monumental aspects of classical antiquity – vases, urns, painted

plaques and opulent dinner services decorated with the accoutrements of imperial rule. This design of 1802 is for an ice-urn; although the form is very much in keeping with the factory's preferences of the time, the decoration seems relatively restrained.

Styles IMPERIAL

The intimate relationship of the decorative arts in France with central sources of patronage – court and aristocracy – had been profoundly disrupted by the Revolution. Under Napoleon, however, that relationship was restored; the luxury crafts were revitalized and a number of the Parisian *ateliers* reopened workshops which had flourished under the Ancien Régime, returning to the traditions of excellence of the eighteenth century. Conquest also facilitated the spread of French styles and goods throughout Europe; Napoleon wanted economic as well as military hegemony for France. Specific influences affected style and design; military success in Egypt was followed by the incorporation of Egyptian motifs into a broadly Neoclassical design repertory. Publications such as Denon's *Voyage dans la Basse- et Haute-Egypte* (1802) reflected a widespread interest in ancient cultures – Greek, Roman, Etruscan, Oriental, as well as Egyptian – which in turn led to much more literal translations of the styles of antiquity than had been the case in the eighteenth century.

Under the Consulate (1799–1804) the Louis-Seize styles did linger for a time, especially in furniture-making, partly due to the continuing use of the engraved designs of such as Delafosse as models. However, under the influence of both Napoleon and the future Empress, changes began to appear which would eventually lead to the fully realized Empire style. One of the most important and influential works of the period was the decoration of the Château de la Malmaison by Percier and Fontaine, with furniture by the Jacob brothers. Parts of the château, first acquired in 1799, were later refurbished by the same designers and cabinet-makers in a style which we can regard as definitive Empire. The Empress's bedroom, for instance, was styled as a classical pavilion of red cloth, embroidered in gold, and supported by delicate gilt wood columns. Beside the *lit à l'antique*, with its single headboard flanked by gilt-winged forms, stood a *saut de lit*, bearing a basin and jug in Sèvres porcelain, and a *guéridou* with a base of three winged lions and a marble top.

The importance of Imperial patronage in the development of the applied arts cannot be overestimated. Published designs, such as those by Percier, Fontaine and de la Mésangère, inevitably reflected the massive programme of refurbishment undertaken by the Imperial family. These were then used by cabinet-makers and interior designers as models for the rooms they were creating for private middle-class patrons, lending a peculiar homogeneity to design at all levels. This in turn inspired a return to the traditional values of fine workmanship, excellent materials, and care and refinement of detail and finish. The efforts made by the designers and craftsmen of the Garde-Meubles Impérial were quite stupendous. The Tuileries, the palaces of the Élysée and of Prince Eugène de Beauharnais in Paris, as well as the châteaux of Fontainebleau and Compiègne, and the Trianon were all refurnished. Orders were executed by the leading cabinet-makers and bronze-sculptors, bringing prosperity and a new brilliance to the traditional crafts.

The fashions of the Empire period proper did not differ signally from those of the Consulate. Even under the Directoire the Jacobs, for instance, were already designing pieces which incorporated features of the Empire style. What tended to happen, however, was for design to become gradually heavier and more obviously 'Imperial' as the period wore on. The gilt-bronze mounts, for instance, which embellished so much furniture, became coarser. Supports of, say, console tables were carved in the form of classical and mythological fauna, replacing the architectural elements – columns and pilasters – of previous years; *commodes* and drop-front *sécretaires* abounded, with mounts of motifs taken from classical antiquity applied to front and side panels. Initially, chairs often retained the scroll-back of the 'Etruscan' style, but the rectangular back, sometimes surmounted by a pediment, became the norm in the later years of the Napoleonic period.

The style created by the Imperial designers, Percier and Fontaine, made itself felt in other areas of the applied arts. Martin-Guillaume Biennais (1764–1843) produced silver and bronze to their designs, including *nécessaires* specifically for Napoleon. The silk factories of Lyons produced material designed for the new Imperial residences; Jean-François Bony (1760–1828), a painter and pupil of the Rococo designer Philippe de Lasalle, became supplier of silk to the Empress Josephine, for whom he made a coronation robe and supplied fabrics for the refurbishment of Malmaison. Indeed, the lavish use of textiles in interior decoration was a notable feature of the Empire style. Strongly patterned silks and velvets were swept over pelmets and bed frames, while small rooms were sometimes given the appearance of pavilions. This effect was imitated by wallpaper manufacturers and wallpaper now began to replace wall-painting in interior schemes.

Although the Empire style was specifically associated with Napoleon and was spread across Europe by his conquests, it did persist in France during the years of Restoration and even to the July Monarchy. Fontaine and the Jacobs were still the recipients of official patronage and the prints of de la Mésangère were still being published. Generally, however, taste became more eclectic, with the appearance of a Gothic element and the emergence of the so-called *style duchesse de Berry*, which utilized light woods inlaid with darker ones. This penchant for *bois clair* was succeeded by the return to popular taste of darker woods – mahogany, ebony and oak, These were sometimes used to make strangely hybrid articles of furniture which incorporated panels of glass or porcelain to offset the severe effect of the wood. In other applied arts the traditional factories continued to supply the growing middle-class market but, as in Great Britain, there was a decline in craftsmanship as the introduction of industrial methods made itself felt.

---

pages 118-119
This engraving of a middle-class Empire interior, *La Perfection du Désordre*, shows a number of interesting style features of the period, including a *lit en bateau*, with gilt-bronze mounts, and a chair with legs *en sabre*.

page 120
Charles Christofle (1815–63) bought the French rights in 1842 to the electroplating process patented by the Elkington company in England; this engraving shows a silver-plating workshop in the Christofle factory.

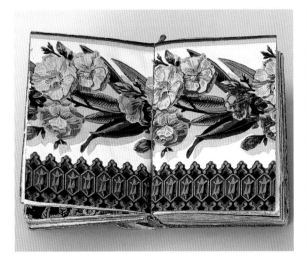

121

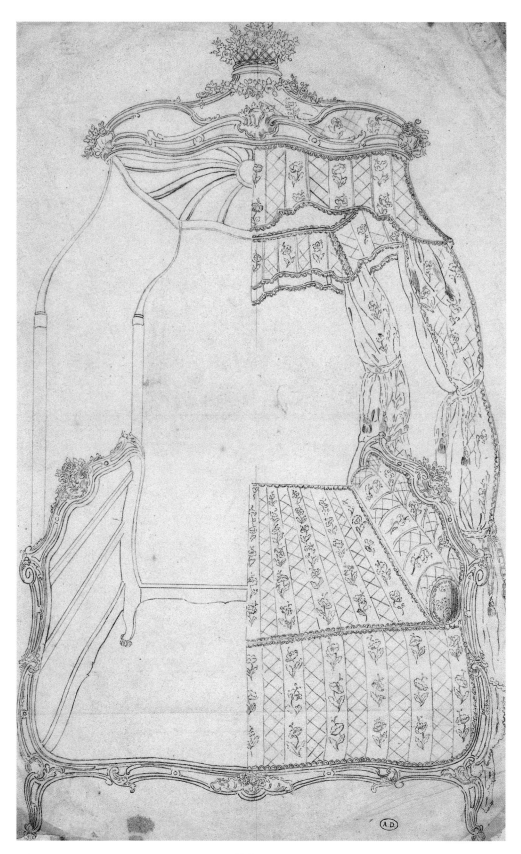

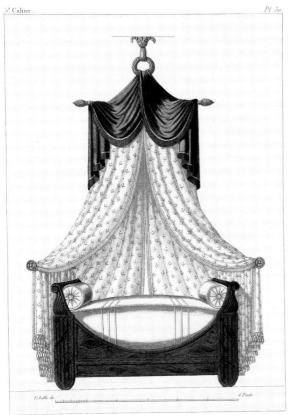

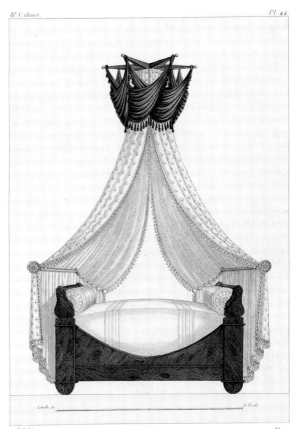

Echelle de _____ 6 Pieds

Echelle de _____ 6 Pieds

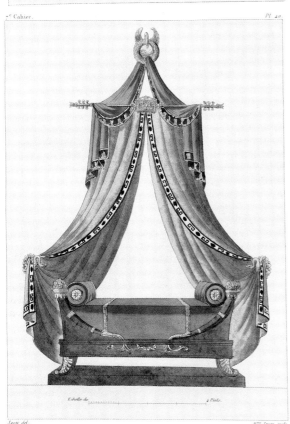

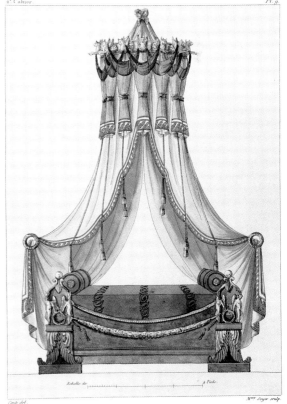

Echelle de _____ 4 Pieds.

Echelle de _____ 4 Pieds.

Santi del.   Mᵐᵉ Soyer sculp.

Ponti del.   Mᵐᵉ Soyer sculp.

Lit à Tente.

Lit à Dome.

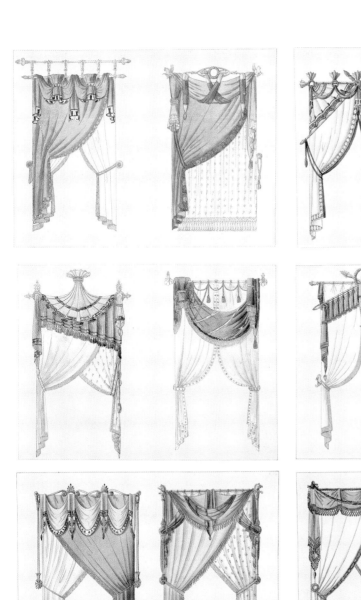
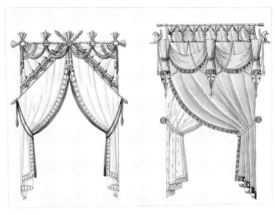
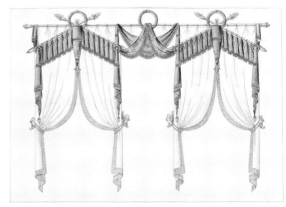
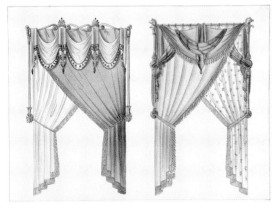

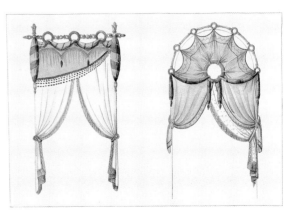

129

Nº 3814. Doré f 7.   Encrier de bureau.

Nº 3815. Doré f 3 50 Encrier de bureau

Nº 3817. Encrier à côtes Doré f 6. 75.

Nº 3816. Sablier Doré f 3. 60.

Nº 3710. Encrier soulier Doré f 8.

Nº 3818. Encrier pot courant Doré f 4. 50.

Nº 3819. Encrier Doré f 12.

Nº 3820. Encrier Doré f 6.

Nº 3821. Encrier porte plume Doré f 10.

Nº 3822. Encrier Doré f 4. 50.

130

Nᵒ 3802. Buste Voltaire (f. Colonne). /16   Nᵒ 3803. Veilleuse (f. lent. transparente) Vaire. /45   Ecritoire Nᵒ 3804.   (A.D.)   Picard. /60

Tuys alumette. Nᵒ 3805.   Vialard Nᵒ 3806. Biscuit. /10   Decrotoir Nᵒ 3807. Bleu. /10   Nᵒ 3808. Bougeoir. Biscuit. /21.
Vaire. /9.

Nᵒ 3720. Tasse à bord. Reguier Vaire. /18.   Nᵒ 3809. Tasse à lent. loxotopht. Picard. /18   Nᵒ 3715. Tasse à lent. Picard. /12.

Nᵒ 3514.   (A.D.)   Tasse à feuill. /12.   Picard   Nᵒ 3717. Tasse à lent. /18   Nᵒ 3716. Tasse à bord. Vaire. /12.

B. = 1839. n° 7

Vase Clodion 2e guirlande de fleurs

Batterie de cuisine en fer battu étamé.
Fig.1. Bouilloire de 4¼ l.

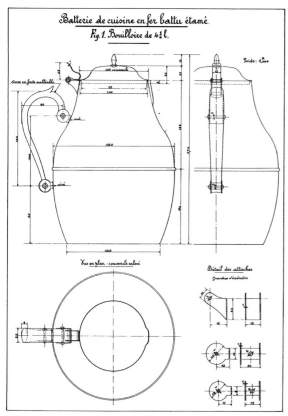

Vue en plan - couvercle enlevé

Détail des attaches
Grandeur d'exécution

Batterie de cuisine.
— FILTRES À CAFÉ —
Fig.4. Filtre de 1 l ½.
(cuivre rouge étamé intérieurement).

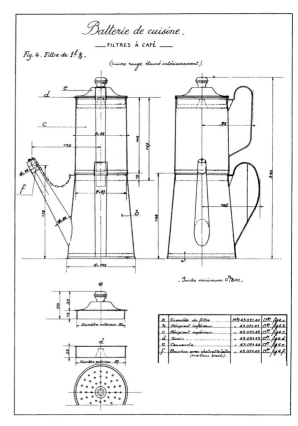

_ Poids minimum 0,800 _

A	Ensemble du filtre	H^lle 43.021.40	D^tt fig.4
b	Récipient inférieur	« 43.021.41	D^tt fig.4.b
c	Récipient supérieur	« 43.021.42	D^tt fig.4.c
d	Tamis	« 43.021.43	D^tt fig.4.d
e	Couvercle	« 43.021.44	D^tt fig.4.e
f	Bouchon avec chaînette laiton (maillons brasés).	« 43.021.45	D^tt fig.4.f

Poterie en porcelaine blanche
Fig.1. Pot pour bain-marie (copette).

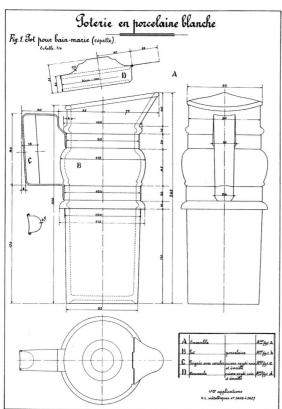

A	Ensemble	A^me fig.1.a
B	Pot porcelaine	A^me fig.1.b
C	Tuyaie avec cercles cuivre oxydé noir et émaillé	A^me fig.1.c
D	Couvercle cuivre oxydé noir et émaillé	A^me fig.1.d

1res applications
V.L. métalliques n° 3606 à 5627

Batterie de cuisine. Echelle ⅕.
Casseroles à manche en fer sans couvercle
Fig 1 Casserole de 27/10
Fig 2 Casserole de 25/15
Fig 3 Casserole de 20/15
Fig 4 Casserole de 18/10
Fig 5 Casserole de 16/10

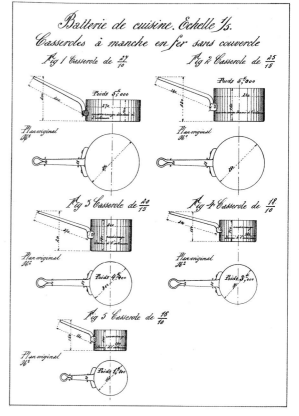

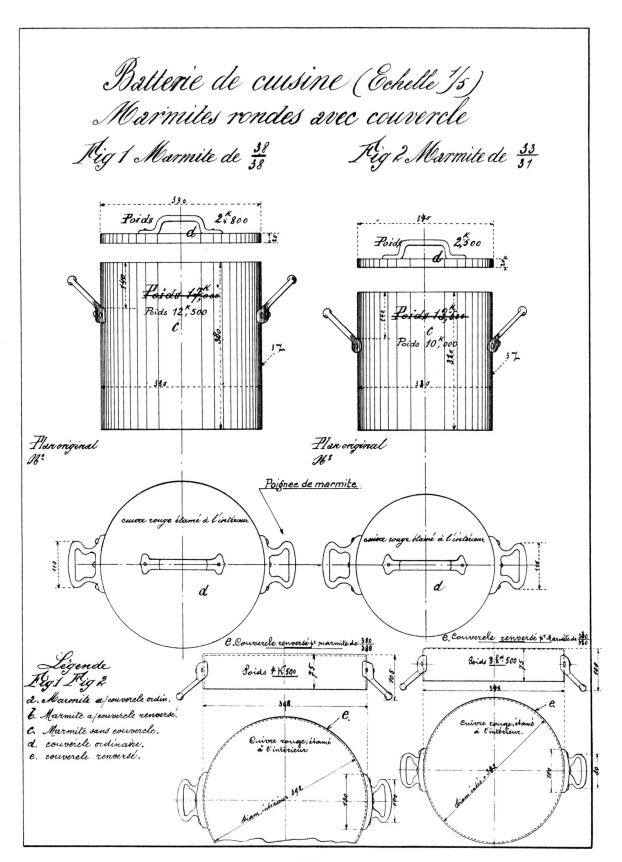

Batterie de cuisine (Echelle ⅕)
Marmites rondes avec couvercle

Fig 1 Marmite de $\frac{38}{38}$ Fig 2 Marmite de $\frac{33}{31}$

Poids 2ᵏ,800

Poids 14ᵏ,000
Poids 12ᵏ,500
c

Poids 2ᵏ,500
d

Poids 12ᵏ,500
Poids 10ᵏ,000
c

Plan original
N°

Plan original
N°

cuivre rouge étamé à l'intérieur

Poignée de marmite

cuivre rouge étamé à l'intérieur

d

d

Légende
Fig 1 Fig 2
a. Marmite a/couvercle ordin.
b. Marmite a/couvercle renversé.
c. Marmite sans couvercle.
d. couvercle ordinaire.
e. couvercle renversé.

e. Couvercle renversé p. marmite de $\frac{380}{380}$

Poids 4ᵏ,500

e. Couvercle renversé p. marmite de $\frac{380}{380}$

Poids 3ᵏ,500

Cuivre rouge; étamé
à l'intérieur
e.

diam intérieur 392

cuivre rouge; étamé
à l'intérieur
e.

diam intér 342

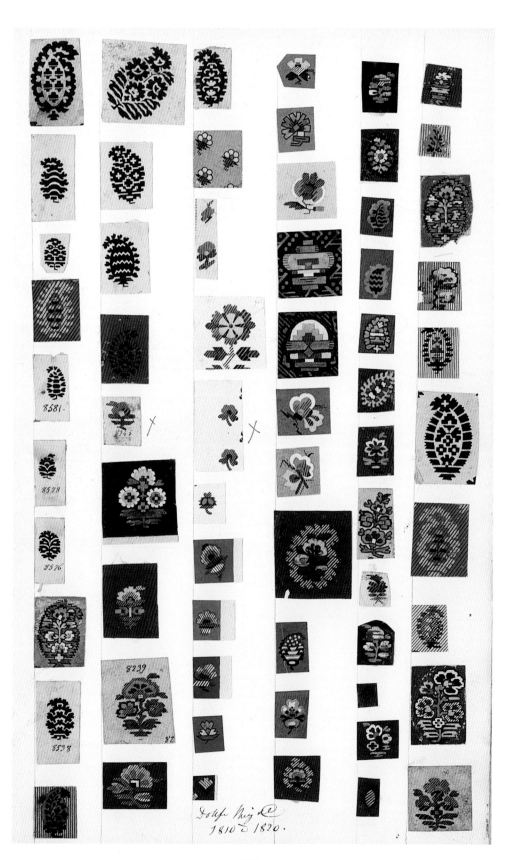

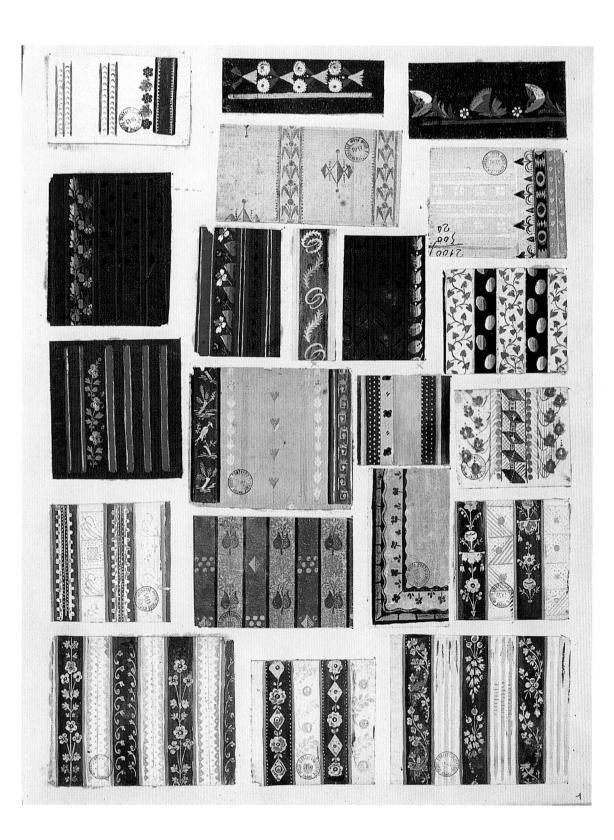

7294.

Théières d'Argent à Anse d'Ebène. Porte-

Liqueur en Argent, Casses en Vermeil.

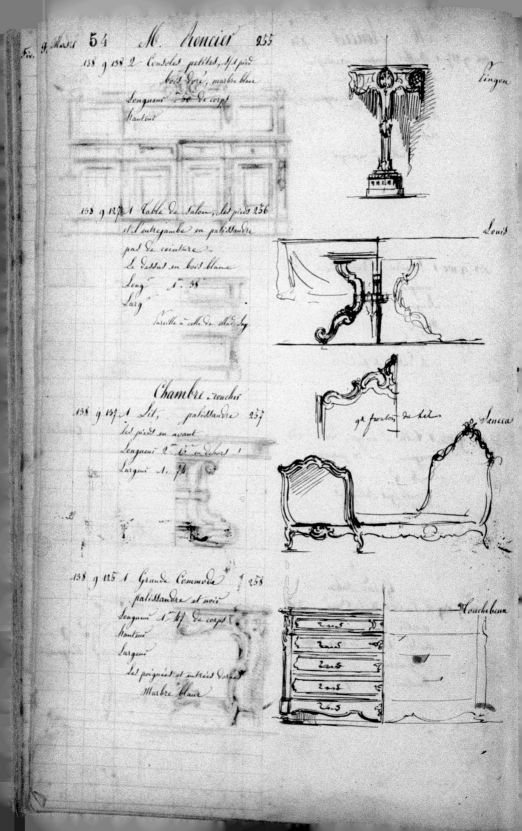

138 g 158 2 Consoles petites, 3/4 pied
             bois doré, marbre blanc
Longueur 1ere de corps
Hauteur

Lingon

138 g 127 1 Table de Salon, les pieds   256
             et l'entrejambe en palissandre
             pas de ceinture
             Le dessus en bois blanc
             Long   1. 38
             Larg
                   Pareille à celle de Mad. Ley

Louis

Chambre à coucher

138 g 137 1 Lit,   palissandre   257
             les pieds en avant
             Longueur 2e 1ere en dehors
             Largeur 1. 74

9e fronton de lit.

Seneca

138 g 125 1 Grande Commode   1 258
             palissandre et noir
Longueur 1. 41 de corps
Hauteur
Largeur
             Les poignées et entrées dorés
             Marbre blanc

Touchebeau

188 9 126 2 petites Commodes Chiffonniers
palissandre et noir
Longueur
Largeur
Hauteur
Les poignées et entrées dorés
Marbre blanc

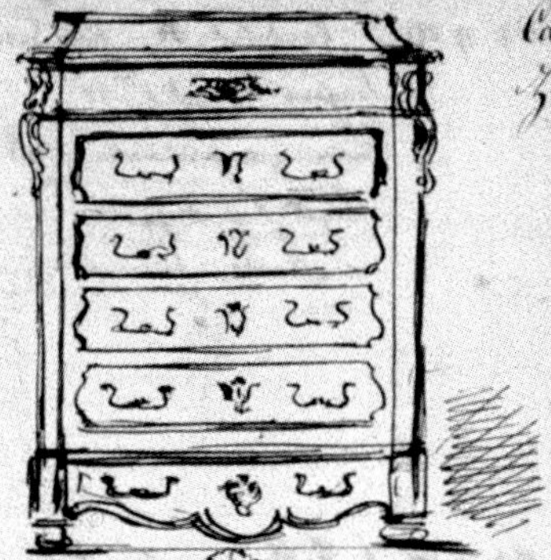

Carra
Zellner

188 9 135 1 Armoire à glace   260
paliss. et bord noir
Hauteur   2. 33
Largeur de corps 1.
Deux petits motifs, bronze doré
La moulure d'encadrement de la
glace sera dorée — le bois même

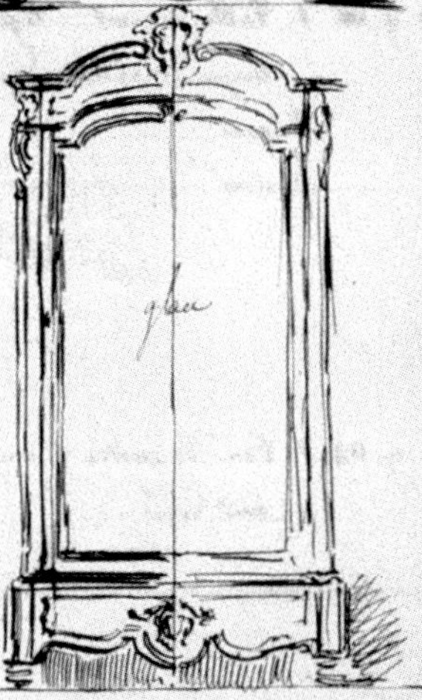

glace

Schmitz

Petit salon

188 9 105 1 Petit Bureau, palissandre 261
Longueur   0, 95
Hauteur
Profondeur

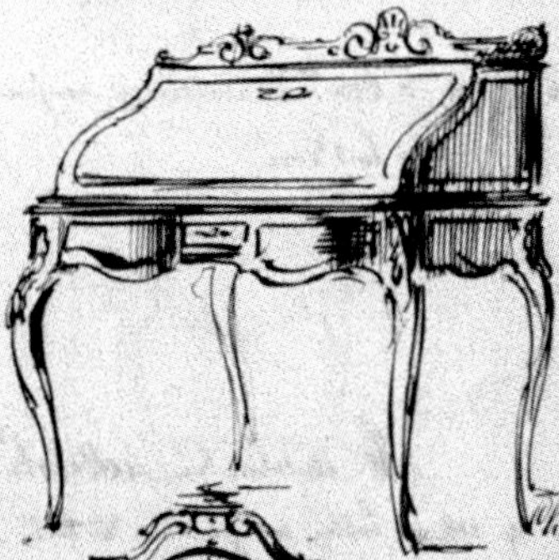

Bailly

188 9 110 2 Bibliothèques, paliss. 262
Largeur de corps   0, 90
Profondeur   . 45
Hauteur, non compris le socle 2. 45
L'intérieur en velours.

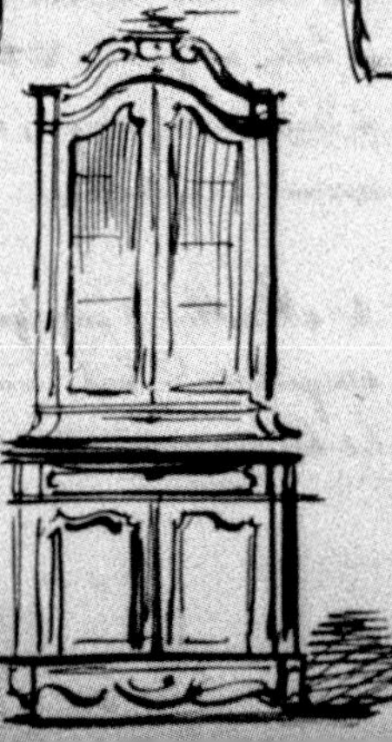

Chevallier
et son fils

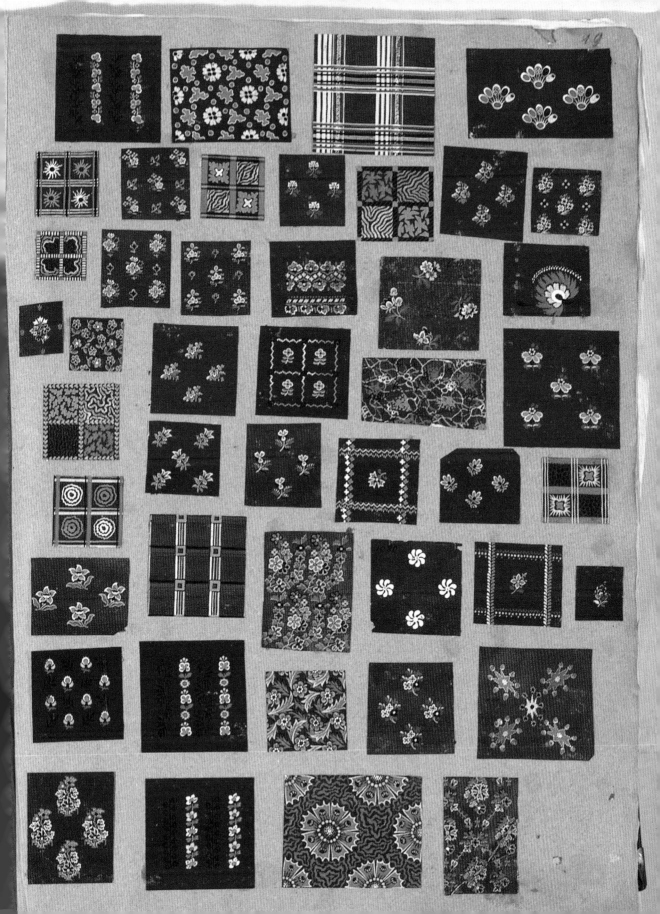

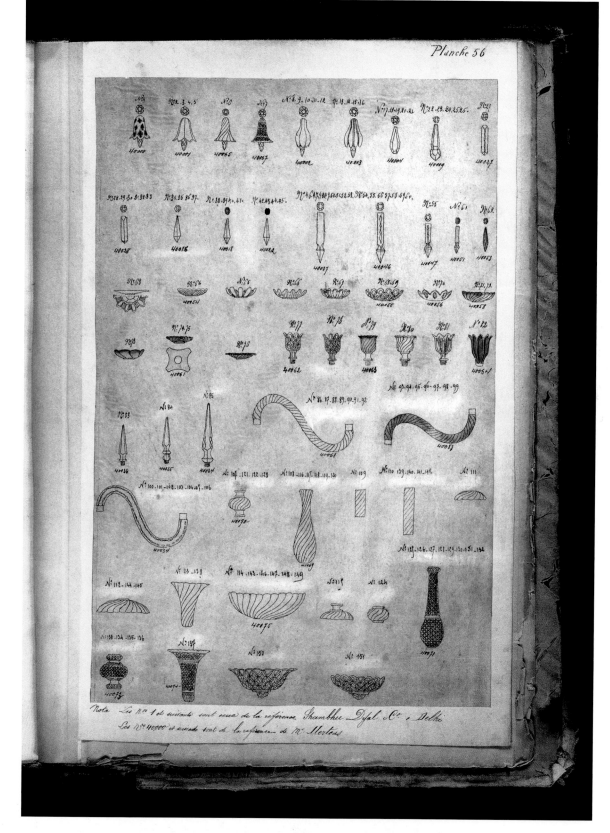

LT. 424 à 162 Lumières

70 sur le grand D.

75

№ 1239

№ 1240

№ 1241

№ 1142

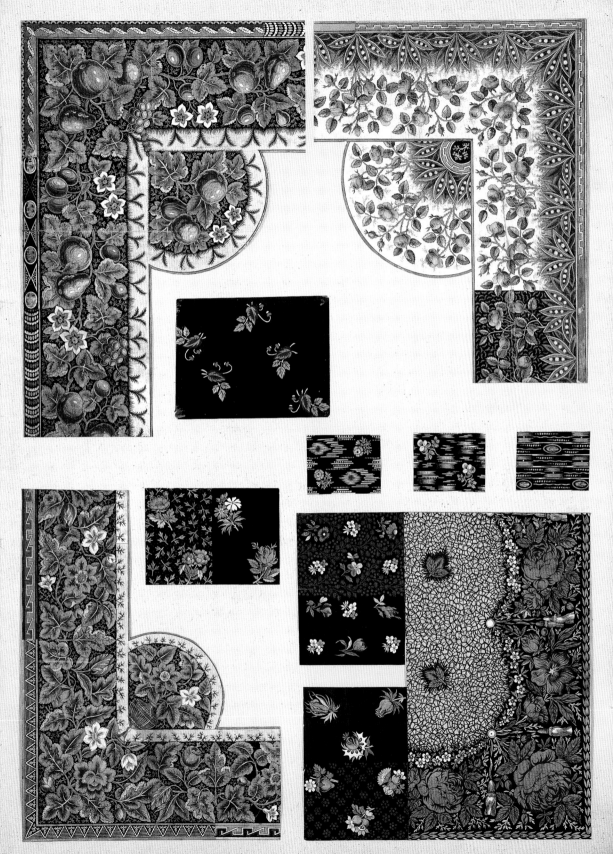

projet de service de table, Vues pittoresques de Suisse. 1840.

4
Styles
IMPERIAL

page 121

It was during the early part of the nineteenth century that wallpaper began to replace to a significant degree painting and panelling as a means of covering internal walls. These sample books of paper and borders were originally produced by the Manufacture Dufour in Paris; they are now held in the collection of the Musée du Papier Peint, Rixheim.

page 122

For the affluent patrons of the cabinet-makers of early nineteenth-century Paris there was an abundance of published sources to help guide their taste in furniture and upholstery. These usually took the form of engravings, published in series. The most successful collection of designs was Pierre de la Mésangère's *Collection de Meubles et Objets de Goût*, which appeared from the end of the eighteenth century to the eighteen-thirties, thus charting in its four hundred or so plates the development of furniture and furnishing from the Directoire, through Consulate and Empire, to the Restoration. Some of de la Mésangère's early plates illustrated chairs very similar to those made in the workshops of Georges Jacob, notably ones with scrolled or curved back-rests and *sabre* legs.

page 123

As the nineteenth century progressed, the more strict Neoclassicism, which had to a large extent been carried over into the Empire style, began to be relaxed. New, hybrid forms appeared in furniture designs, often with a more obvious regard for comfort in the form of such features as rounded backs and a concern for the body in relaxation. These projects for armchairs, in black ink and watercolour, are from a reference album in the Musée des Arts Décoratifs in Paris.

pages 124–125

Early nineteenth-century wallpaper manufacturers clearly tried to imitate the grander effects of the Empire style, with its distinct predilection for textile effects. These two examples, block-printed in fourteen colours, were found superimposed the one on the other in an interior in the centre of Strasbourg. The first (*p. 125*) dates from *c.* 1810–15, while the second, which bears the manufacturer's name of Jean Zuber et Cie, dates from approximately ten years later. Both are in the collection of the Musée du Papier Peint, Rixheim.

page 126

As the Empire style gradually lost its appeal to contemporary taste during the eighteen-twenties and thirties, designers and decorators began to plunder the styles of the past. This pencil sketch on tracing paper of a *lit à la polonaise* by the designer/decorator Aimé Chenevard has a distinctly mid eighteenth-century look, even though it was in fact executed around 1830. The original drawing is in the collection of the Musée des Arts Décoratifs, Paris.

page 127

One of the most representative forms of the bed in the late Neoclassical style was the *lit en bateau*, in which the head and foot boards were of equal height. A feeling of opulence was enhanced by the extensive use of draperies, swept up over the bed in elaborate canopy forms, as in those illustrated here: *lit à couronne et à tente*, *lit à étoile*, *lit à tente* and *lit à dôme*. The sides and ends of the beds were sometimes decorated with gilt-bronze mounts which stood out strongly against the essential simplicity of the basic shape. In well-to-do houses, the bed would probably be the centre-piece of a whole tableau, which could include night-tables,

4

Styles
IMPERIAL

candelabra and wall-hangings. One famous example of the *lit en bateau* was that belonging to the society beauty, Juliette Récamier, whose house was partly decorated by Charles Percier, with furniture made by Jacob.

page 128

A design for 'lace' wallpaper, dating from 1831; in the sumptuousness of such designs we can already see the developing taste for comfort which characterized middle-class interior decoration for much of the nineteenth century. This design by Koechlin-Ziegler was manufactured by J. Zuber et Cie; it was exhibited at the Paris Exposition des Produits de l'Industrie in 1834. The sample illustrated is in the collection of the Musée du Papier Peint in Rixheim.

page 129

Another influential publication, which very much imitated the form and style of the *Collection de Meubles et Objets de Goût*, was M. Santi's *Modèles de meubles et de décorations intérieures pour l'ameublement* in seventy-two plates, published in Paris in 1828. It shows, typically, curtain arrangements in what might be called a late Empire style.

pages 130–131

Objects for the growing middle-class of the post-Empire period, from porcelain ink-wells to cups and saucers; these pages are reproduced from a pattern book of the Manufacture Dagoty et Honoré, now held in the collection of the Musée des Arts Décoratifs, Paris. The original designs are in ink and watercolour.

pages 132–133

The silk workshops of Lyons enjoyed a period of considerable prosperity during the Empire, partly due to the direct patronage of Napoleon. Designs were often elaborate, yet with a sort of formal strength, as in this example (p. 133) taken from a book of sketches dated 1800–1820 in the collection of the Musée des Arts Décoratifs in Paris. The porcelain manufactory of Sèvres was also much patronized by the Emperor, but after 1815 a certain fussiness can be discerned in the design and decoration of pieces; all the formality of the Empire style has disappeared in this project for the decoration of a vase (p. 132) in favour of a self-consciously pretty effect.

pages 134–135

Sheets of detailed trade drawings of professional kitchen equipment. It was during the mid nineteenth century that the habit of dining out in restaurants began to grow among the fashionable Parisian middle-class, another reflection of its growing prosperity.

page 136

This page of textile designs is taken from one of the many swatch-books held by the Musée de l'Impression sur Étoffes; it is dated 1810–1820 and gives us a clear impression of the strong, simple design of the Empire period.

page 137

These goblet designs appeared in the 1840 catalogue of Launay, Hautin & Cie. The original document is now in the Collection of the Juliette K. and Leonard S. Rakow Research Library of the Corning Museum of Glass, New York.

page 138

The Lyons silk industry thrived on the orders for the refurbishment of the Imperial residences during the Napoleonic era. But after the decline of Empire many factories began to manufacture to more floral designs for the new middle-class market; this sample of swatches is probably indicative of the design concerns of the industry at that time. It is reproduced from an original in the collection of the Musée des Tissus, Lyons.

page 139

This project for a dressing-table-cum-writing-desk is reproduced from an album of furniture designs in ink and watercolour held in the collection of the Musée des Arts Décoratifs, Paris.

pages 140–141

Pierre de la Mésangère's publication, the *Collection de Meubles et Objets de Goût,* must have provided the wealthy bourgeoisie of the Empire period with a complete guide to contemporary style and design. These silver and ebony teapots indicate the continuing taste of the early nineteenth century for the elegant fluted lines of Neoclassicism. Similarly, the liqueur tray and decanters are decorated with motifs drawn from classical mythology.

pages 142–143

Even after the fall of Napoleon and the withdrawal of Imperial patronage, the position of Lyons as the European centre of high-quality textile production remained assured by the fineness of the weaving and the elegance of the design, as evidenced by the swatches reproduced from an album in the collection of the Bibliothèque Forney, Paris.

pages 144–145

As the Neoclassical legacy of the Empire began to weaken in the eighteen-thirties, the influence of a burgeoning middle-class began to make itself felt. In terms of taste this was translated into a trend towards eclecticism, especially in furniture and interior decoration. Designers began to borrow features from every style from the Renaissance onwards, but especially from Louis-Quatorze (the designs of Boulle became popular again), Régence, Louis-Quinze and Louis-Seize. One of the leading makers of high-quality revivalist furniture was the firm founded in Paris in 1835 by Alexandre-Georges Fourdinois (1799–1871) and continued until 1887 by his son Henri-Auguste (1830–1907). Both members of the family worked in a variety of styles, from the seventeenth and eighteenth centuries, although the son seems to have eventually settled for a particularly pompous interpretation of Renaissance styles. These pages occur in an order book dated 1845–59, now held in the Bibliothèque Forney in Paris. The designs, especially those of the bed and desk, strongly recall the Louis-Quinze style, while others have simpler lines which suggest an interpretation of Régence models.

pages 146–147

More examples of what domestic design must have looked like during the Empire period; these swatches are reproduced from an album in the collection of the Musée de l'Impression sur Étoffes, Mulhouse. It is dated 1800–1810.

pages 148–149

Originally founded in Lunéville in 1765, the glass producer Baccarat enjoyed a period of especial design distinction and commercial success during the first half of the nineteenth century. It produced crystal tableware and vases, chandeliers and paperweights in a variety of designs and colours. These designs for decorative components in crystal and for a complete 170 candle chandelier are reproduced from documents still in the company archives.

pages 150–151

These freshly coloured pages from albums of textile designs are ample testimony to the continuing vigour of artistry within the French industry during the early nineteenth century. By the mid eighteenth century French block printers had mastered the art of fixing dyes and were able to produce textiles which rivalled those of the Orient in the complexity of their design and the brilliance of their colouring (*see pp. 90–91*).

page 152

These pencil sketches of designs for plate borders are still held by the archives of the Sèvres porcelain manufactory. Dating from *c.* 1840, they show imagery derived from the flora and fauna of the Swiss alps and belong very much to the period during which the factory made wares with elaborate decoration.

Revivalism and REVOLUTION

The dominant trend in taste of the Second Empire (1848–70) was not just middle-class and eclectic, it was positively preda-tory with regard to the past glories of French design. Retailers, abetted by upholsterers who often took over the rôle of coordi-nating whole interiors, began to offer pieces incorporating features borrowed from every style from the Renaissance onwards, but especially from Louis-Quatorze, Louis-Quinze and Louis-Seize. Cabinets made in the grand manner of Boulle became a feature of fashionable *salons*. A number of such pieces were made by Frédéric Roux for the imperial apart-ments in the Tuileries; Roux also found a market for his cabinets in the United States through the furniture business of his brother Alexandre, who had workshops on Broadway, New York.

Although Rococo enjoyed some popularity, especially among wealthier patrons, it was the Louis-Seize style which dominated by the end of Napoleon III's reign, partly because the Empress Eugénie identified herself with the Neo-classical tastes of Marie-Antoinette to inspire what became known as the *style Louis-Seize impératrice*. Many of these pieces were of high quality, especially those bought by the prosperous Parisian *bourgeoisie* to furnish their apartments. These latter were very formally structured in their layout: *vestibule*, *salon*, *petit salon* and the *salle à manger* constituted

the main living area. The dining-room would probably be furnished in a heavy, early style, but the *petit salon* would almost certainly be in the lighter Louis-Seize revival style, as would the bedroom. Textiles and draperies proliferated in the form of curtains with swags and trimmings. Given the supremacy of the upholsterer, it is not surprising to find heavily padded furniture appearing: *pouffes*, low armchairs known as *crapauds*, and the variety of settees intended to promote intimate conversation between two or three people: *confidantes à deux places*, *canapés de l'amitié* and the entic-ingly named *indiscrets à trois places*. Chairs and settees were grouped together for conversational exchange, while larger articles of furniture would be placed against walls covered in wallpaper perhaps imitating panelling or even the walls of a conservatory.

The progress of the porcelain manufactory of Sèvres in the latter part of the nineteenth century is typical of the changes which eventually revolutionized the applied arts in France. Pastiche was very much the order of the day after the factory was reorganized in 1848, producing imitations of eighteenth-century French and Meissen patterns. Later, Chinese and Japanese models were reproduced. But a turning-point in the manufactory's fortunes was reached in 1887 with the appoint-ment of Joseph-Théodore Deck (1823–91) as director, the first potter to hold the position. From then, the Sèvres design policy became much more adventurous. New materials, including a stoneware and a softer paste, were adopted and, by the late eighteen-nineties, a distinctly Art Nouveau style had been embraced. Various of the factory's products in this style were exhibited at the Paris 1900 exhibition – just one example of the emergence of the applied arts from the lack of direction which had so characterized design during the Second Empire years.

The emergence of the new aesthetic was not easily achieved. Such publications as *La Décoration Intérieure* reproduced designs for complete interiors, first in revivalist, pastiche styles – Russian rooms, Syrian rooms, and so on, then later there do appear transitional styles which finally approach full-blown Art Nouveau. But at the Paris exhibitions of 1878, 1884 and 1889 the furniture exhibited still drew mainly on the styles of the past.

Art Nouveau, as expressed in the work of the School of Nancy (Gallé, Majorelle and Daum) and in that of the Paris designers (Guimard, Colonna, de Feure, to name but a representative few), was undoubtedly a movement of astounding originality in its re-interpretation of familiar forms and artefacts in all branches of the decorative arts. It found inspiration in plant forms, in Oriental art, and in the international design movements which developed specifically as a reaction against the muddle of much of mid nineteenth-century design. The heavy, saturated colours of the Second Empire interior were anathema to the new school; the tones of the new textiles and wallpapers were subdued: pale pink, pale blue, light green and yellow. Yet the very originality of the new aesthetic, in spite of its constant exposure in reviews and plate books, meant that

only a relatively small minority of the middle-class adopted it and revivalist styles continued to be popular, even though they no longer reflected the spirit of the age.

The name most closely associated with this resurgent brilliance in the applied arts was that of a Hamburg dealer and retailer, S. Bing, who had opened a gallery in the Rue de Provence under the name of Art Nouveau in which he sold works of art imported from the Far East. By 1895 he had begun to amass furniture, textiles and objects from the new generation of designers with their collaboration, which were exhibited under the title Salon de l'Art Nouveau, giving the movement a show-case and a name. Its triumph, however, was to come in the Paris exhibition of 1900, where once again the productions of French designers and craftsmen were recognized as the finest in Europe. This pre-eminent position was to be further reinforced during the three decades which followed the exhibition.

---

pages 158-159
A late nineteenth-century garden room, complete with *treillage* effects; although the general effect is distinctly revivalist, note the hints of curvilinear Art Nouveau in the chair backs and arms.

page 160
The eight-colour printing machine of the Gillou & Thorailler factory, Paris, 1867; this image of wallpaper printing was reproduced in the report on the Exposition Universelle of 1867.

VENDREDI   11 NOVEMBRE 1831

La Gazette de France.

L'ÉTOILE GAZETTE DE FRANCE donne les Nouvelles étrangères 24 heures avant les autres journaux de Paris, et les Nouvelles officielles en même temps que le Moniteur

NOUVELLES ÉTRANGÈRES.

ANGLETERRE. — *Londres, 7*

(Par voie extraordinaire.)

après avoir exercé ses ravages à Alexandrie pendant 56 jours, a totalement cessé. On dit que 30,000 personnes ont succombé à cette affreuse

— A Hambourg, jusqu'au 28 octobre, en compte, sur 500 personnes atteintes du choléra, 275 morts.
— La conférence a suspendu ses délibérations sur les limites de la Grèce à cause de l'assassinat du comte Capo-d'Istrias.   (Globe.)

POLOGNE.

QUINZE CENTIMES LE NUMÉRO   Jeudi 3 Janvier 1869

Année — N° 4

L'OPINION NATIONALE

JOURNAL POLITIQUE QUOTIDIEN
PARAISSANT LE SOIR

Adresser tout ce qui concerne la Rédaction à M. Ad. GUÉROULT, Rédacteur en chef, à Paris, rue Coq-Héron, 5. (Affranchir)	Les Abonnements partent des 1er et 15 de chaque mois. Pour l'Étranger, le port en sus suivant les conventions postales.	Adresser tout ce qui concerne l'Administration à M. l'Administrateur, à Paris, rue Coq-Héron, 5. (Affranchir)

40

Les Articles non insérés ne seront pas rendus.

42

BULLETIN DU JOUR.

...ONITEUR UNIVERSEL   14 JANVIER 1875

Bureaux de rédaction : 13, quai Voltaire

...zette Nationale fondée en 1789.

LES MANUSCRITS   DÉPARTE...   Numéro 20 centimes

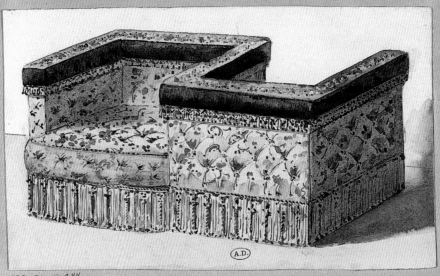

76

CD 5399 B 44

CD 5399 B 45

CD 5399 46

Sond de Remeny.or

164

E. Poirier

(A.D.)

CD 5399 B 56

E. Poirier

(A.D.)

CD 5399 B 57

E. Poirier

(A.D.)

CD 5399 B 58

Poirier fils

(A.D.)

CD 5399 B 59

CD 5399 B 60

(A.D.)

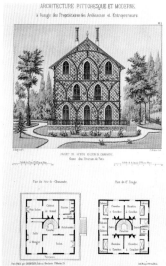

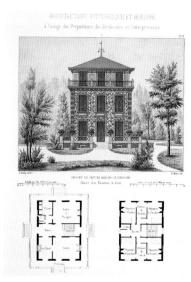

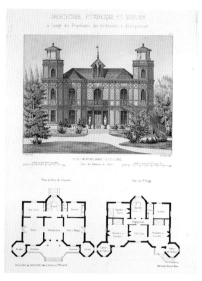

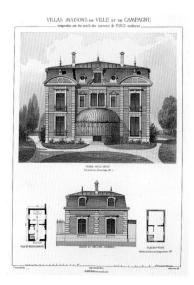

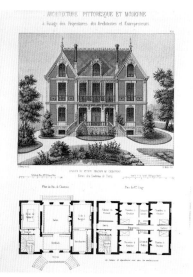

L.Leblanc Arch.del.

Echelle de

PLAN DU REZ-DE-CHAUSSÉE.

Echelle de

PLAN DU 1ER ÉTAGE.

Walter lith.

A LÉVY fils, Editeur, rue de Seine 29.

Imp. Becquet, Paris.

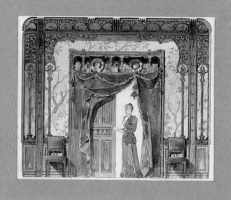

G. Felix Lenoir
mois d'Août 1889.

Projet de Vitraux - Émaux sur verre Anglais

t - Ferraud . Arch.¹ M.ʳ Mizard .

pour le Jardin d' Hiver. Frise en verre decoupé —

C. Pizzagalli 1892

Pl. IV.   POMPEI   fouilles de 1836.

L. Richer pin. e dir.   Richter e C. Napoli   V. Loria dis.

un mètre
Déposé

MAISON D'ARIANNA OU DES CHAPITEAUX COLORÉS

G. Rémon.

E. Thézard fils, Éditeur à Dourdan (S.-et-O.)

Lith. DELAMOTTE, Paris.

INTÉRIEUR INDIEN

HOURCQ & ITHOURBURU
58,Rue de la Chaussée d'Antin,58.
ATELIERS DE DORURE SUR BOIS.

BOIS DORÉ

Pl 8

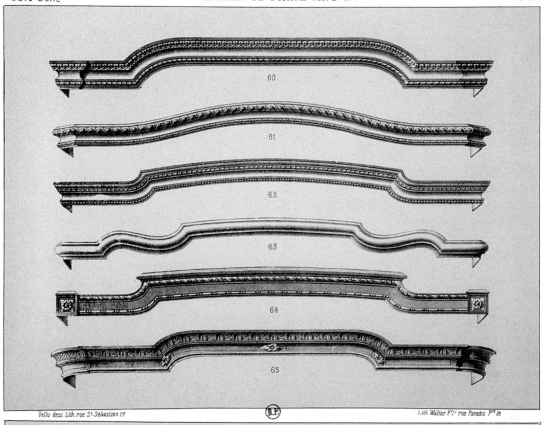

Vellu dess. Lith. rue St-Sébastien 17.   B.F.   Lith Walter Frs rue Paradis Pre 28

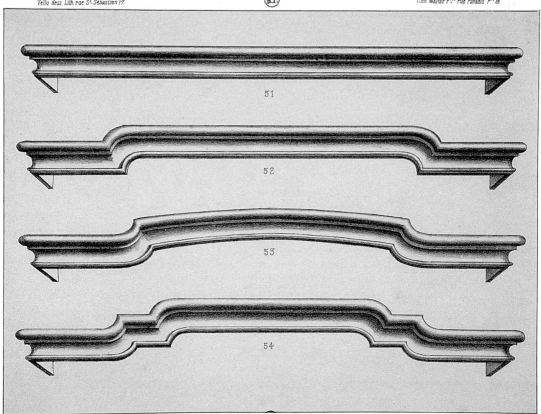

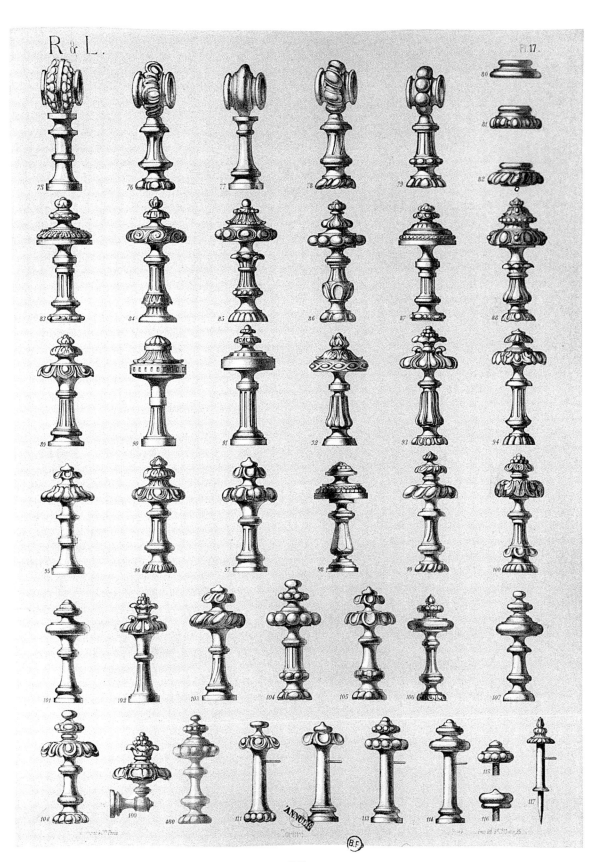

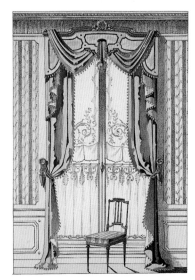

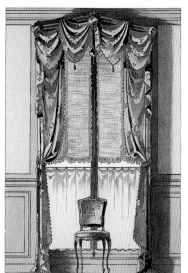

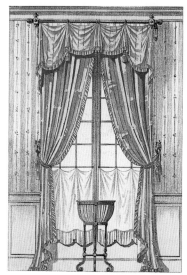

L'EXPOSITION

Journal de l'Industrie et des Arts utiles

par Le Bouteiller rue de la Bourse N.1. à Paris.

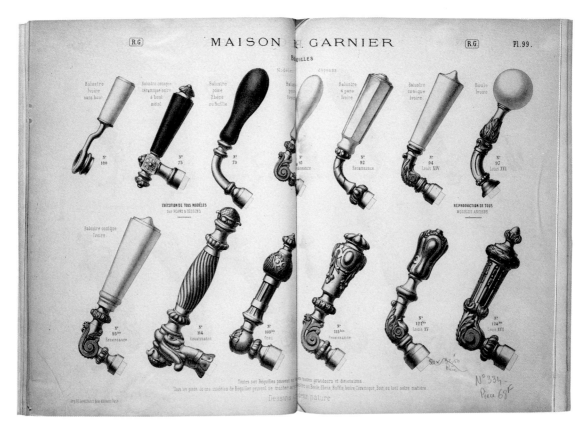

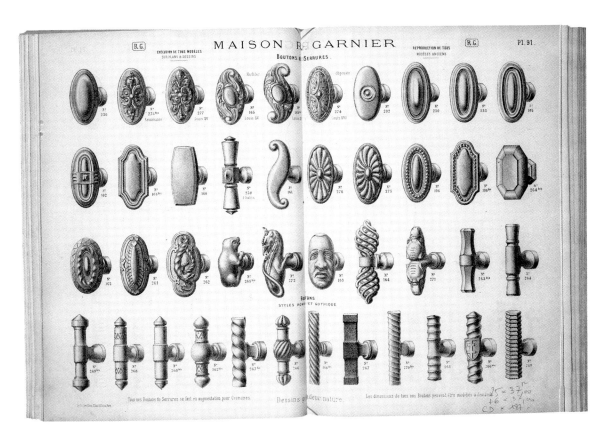

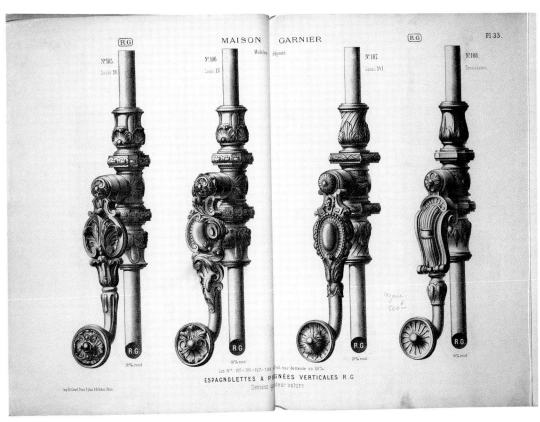

ESPAGNOLETTES A POIGNÉES VERTICALES R.G
Dessins grandeur nature

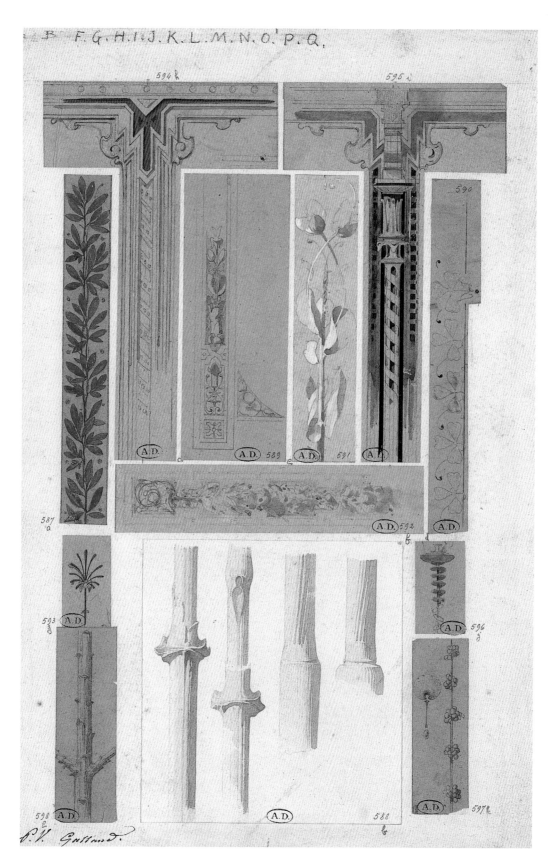

594 h   595 b

590

587 a

A.D.   A.D. 589   A.D. 591   A.D.   A.D.

A.D. 592

593 A.D.

A.D. 596

598 A.D.   A.D.   588   597 b

P.V. Galland.

grandeur naturelle

B

A

A

A

C

D

Énné

Énné

Énné

E

E

E

E gros dans le bois

AA. d'après les petites branches qui entourent le bouquet de lilas mars 1849

grandeur naturelle

d'après une petite branche de lilas

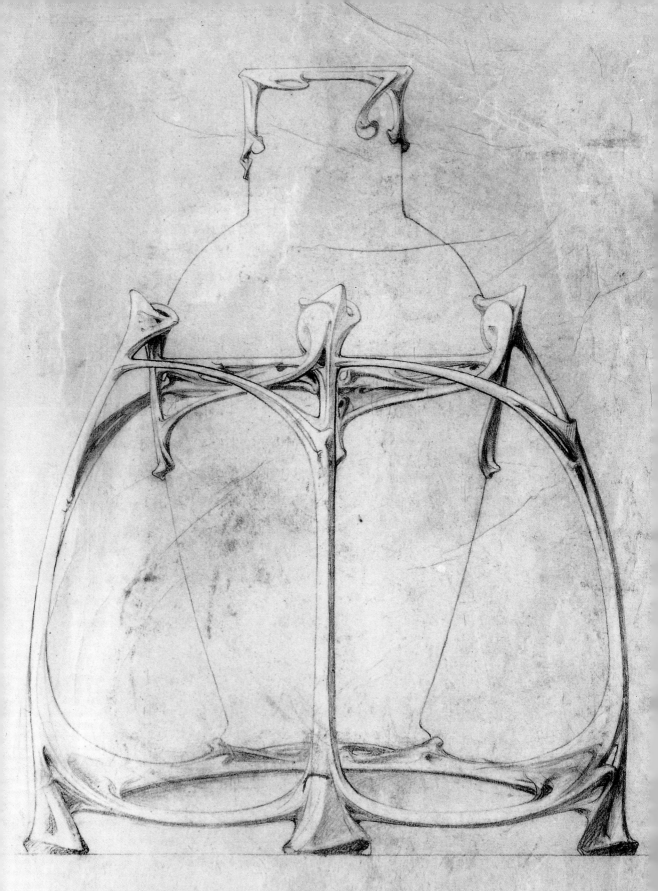

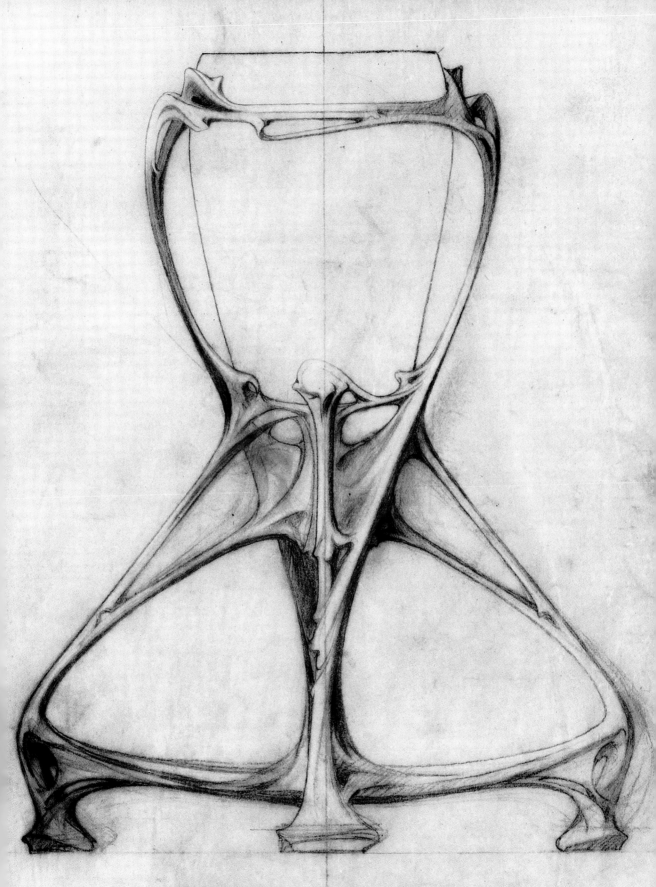

No 2.05

189   N° 80-05

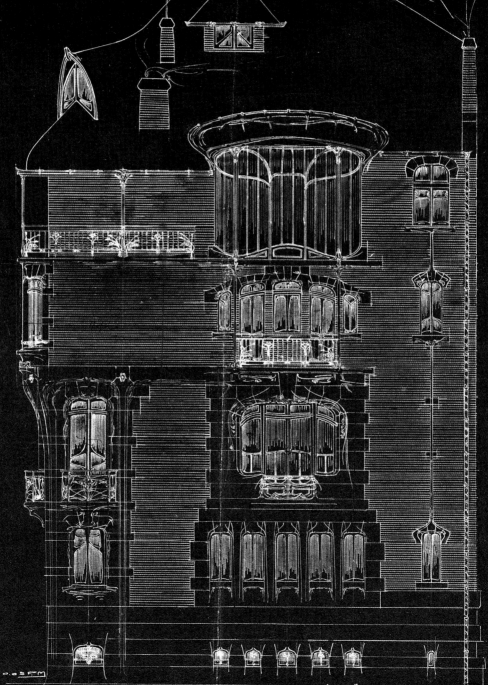

HOTEL GUIMARD

FACADE: VILLA FLORE

PROPRIÉTÉ   122. RUE MOZART

ÉCHELLE 0.02 P.M.

DRESSÉ PAR L'ARCHITECTE SOUSSIGNÉ
PARIS LE   19

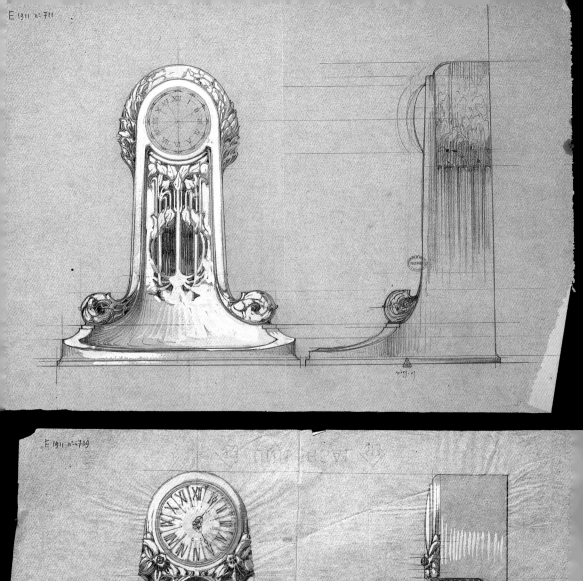

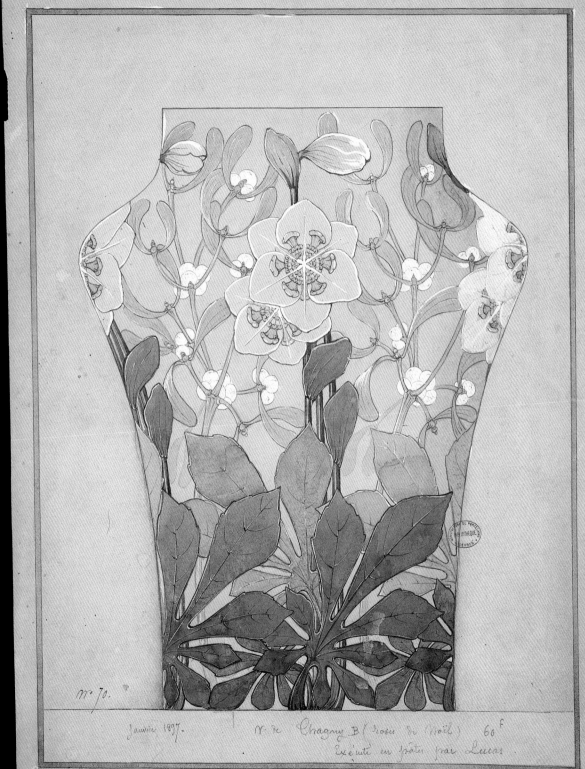

Janvier 1897.   V. de Chagny B (rose de Noël)   60ᶠ

                                       Exécuté en pâte par Lucas.

Eugénie Vaillancourt
Mᵐᵉ Dethmont

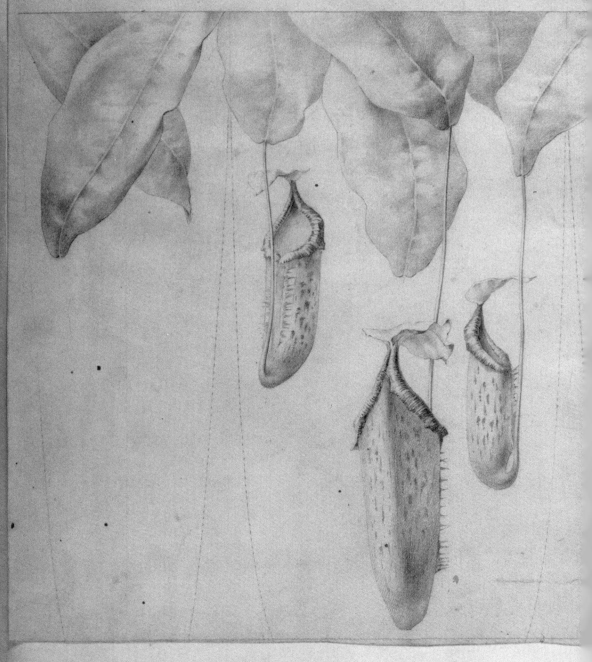

Népenthès

2242 à 280 z.

250 z.

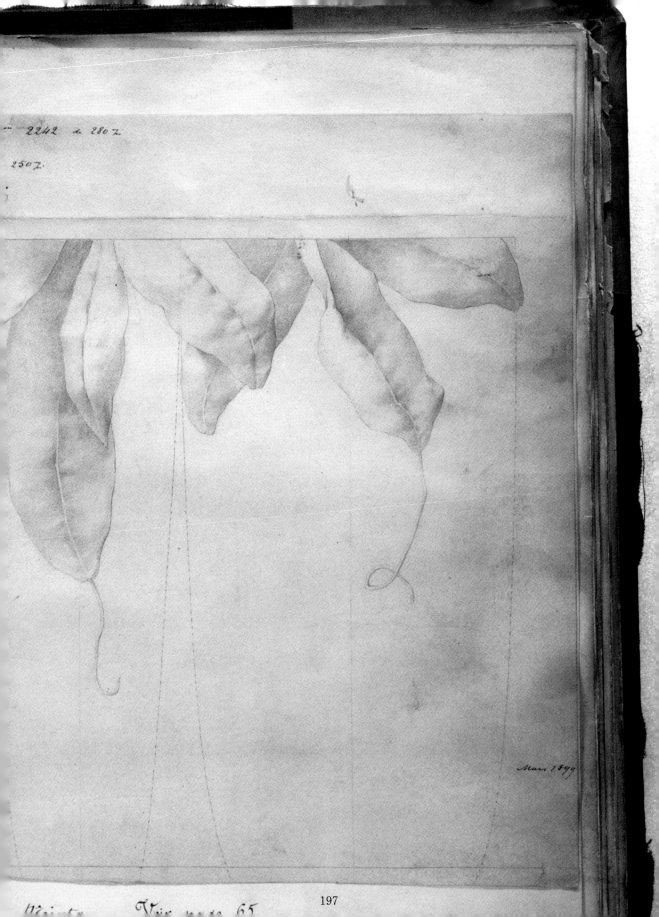

Mars 1899

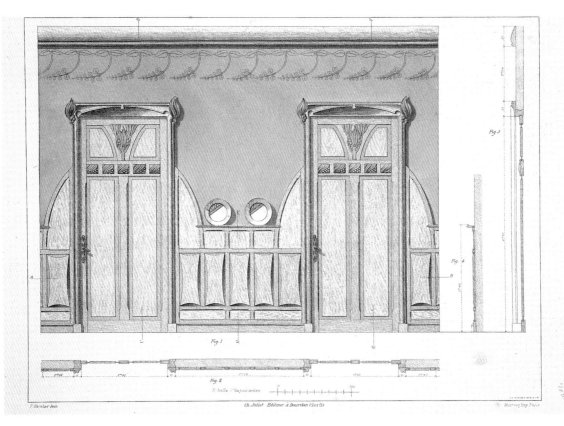

F. Bernhes dess.

Ch. Juliot Editeur à Dourdan (S.et O.)

Monrocq Imp. Paris

Fig. 1

Fig. 2

Fig. 3

Fig. 4

Echelle 5 %m pour mètre

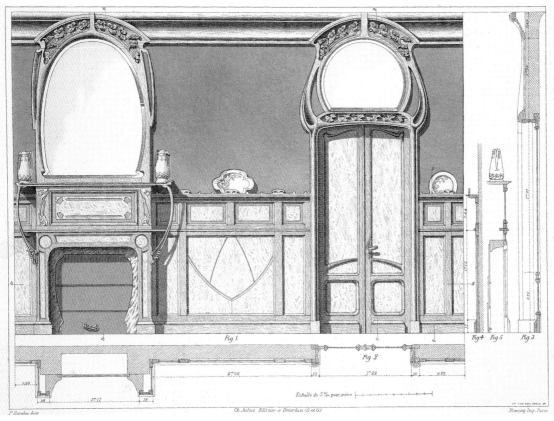

F. Bernhes dess.

Ch. Juliot Editeur à Dourdan (S.et O.)

Monrocq Imp. Paris

Fig. 1

Fig. 2

Fig. 3

Fig. 4

Fig. 5

Echelle de 5 %m pour mètre

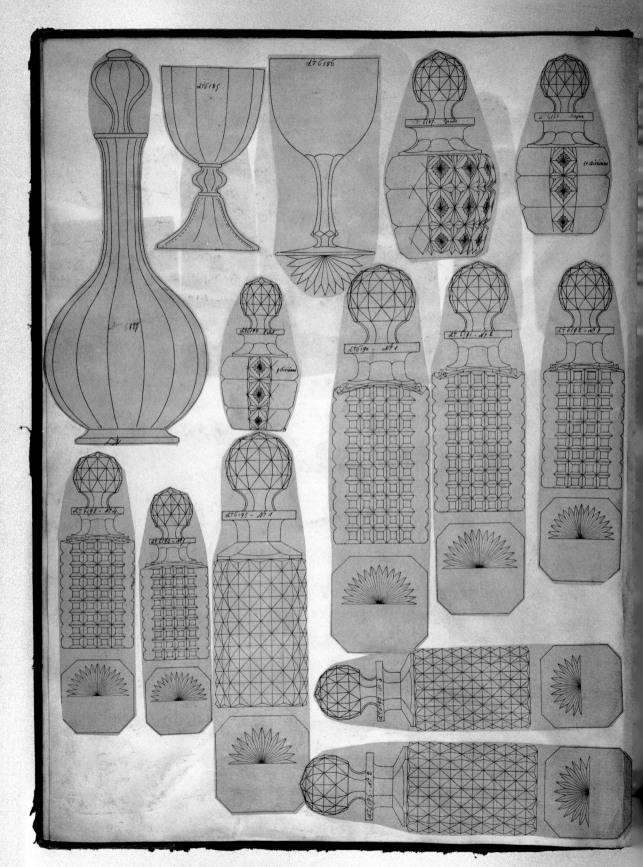

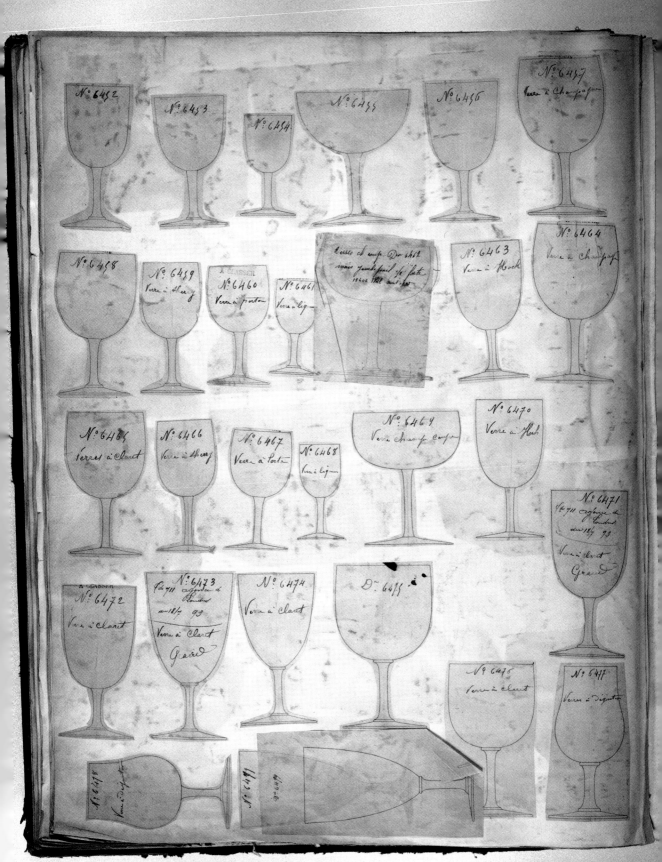

face du bec

Vue de la face droite de la tasse

Exécuté en Sculpture[...]

202.

Plan de la soucoupe

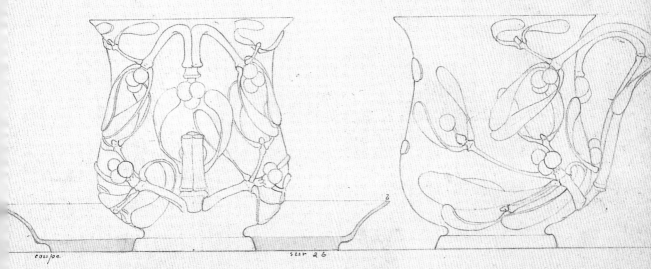

coupe   sur 26

Vue de la face de l'anse.   Vue de la face gauche.

Deviec   appartient au pr no 15 déjà
                                                    à la B

7860-7861 7862 7863 7864 7865
7866 7867 7868 7869 7870
7871 7872 7873 7874 7875
7876 7877 7878 7879 7880
7881 7882 7883 7884 7885
7886 7887 7888 7889 7890
7891 7892 7893 7894 7895
7896 7897 7898 7899 7900
7901 7902 7903 7904 7905
7906 7907 7908 7909 7913 & 7915
7910 7911 7912

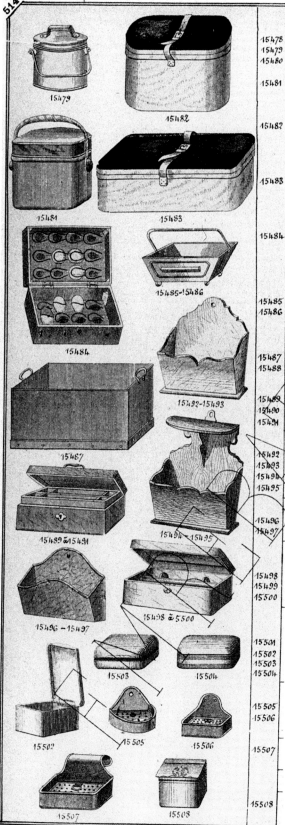

15479
15482
15481 15483
15484
15485-15486
15487
15492-15493
15489 à 15491
15494 - 15495
15496 - 15497
15498 à 5500
15503 15504
15502 15505 15506
15507 15508

15478
15479
15480
15481
15482
15483
15484
15485
15486
15487
15488
15489
15490
15491
15492
15493
15494
15495
15496
15497
15498
15499
15500
15501
15502
15503
15504
15505
15506
15507
15508

(Voir prix pages 655 et 658)

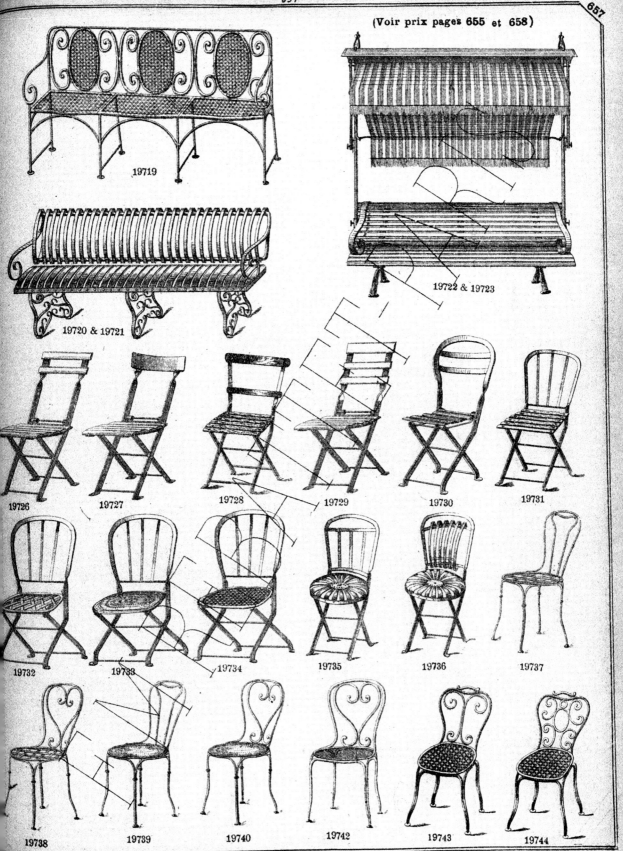

19719

19722 & 19723

19720 & 19721

19726

19727

19728

19729

19730

19731

19732

19733

19734

19735

19736

19737

19738

19739

19740

19742

19743

19744

Nº 61   G. Rault

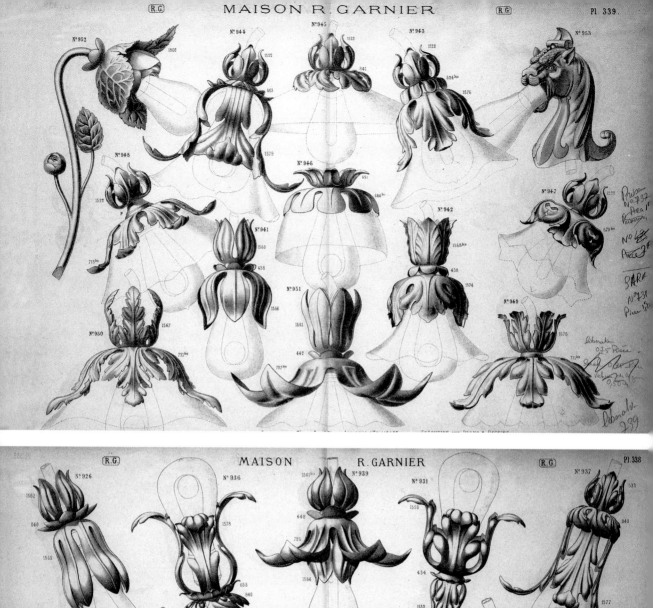

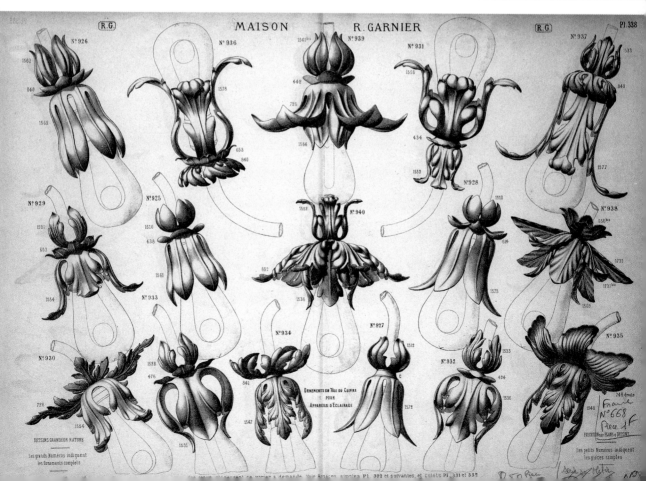

page 161

One of the functions of the Musée du Papier Peint in Rixheim is to act as a centre for the conservation of unusual samples of wallpaper as they become available through the refurbishment or even the demolition of buildings. This extraordinary sample consists of several superimposed layers including an 1831 newspaper and manuscript paper and a final layer (of wallpaper) applied around 1940.

pages 162–163

These pages of swatches are reproduced from albums of woven swatches believed to have been used in Lyons workshops in the latter half of the nineteenth century. The first (*p. 162*), taken from an album dated 1880, is in the collection of the Musée de l'Impression sur Étoffes, Mulhouse. The second (*p. 163*) set of swatches are part of a three-volume record of the production of J. Leroudier, entitled *Soieries de la Fabrique Lyonnaise* and dated 1840– 1900, now held in the

Bibliothèque Forney, Paris.

pages 164–165

Although the leading designers of the latter part of the nineteenth century were exploring new forms in furniture and furnishings, the taste of much of the middle-class still demanded traditional forms and, above all, comfort. These hand-painted designs for sofas and armchairs in crayon, ink and watercolour date from the end of the century and are taken from a pattern book of the Maison Poirier et Rémon.

pages 166–169

With the eclecticism of taste in design of the Second Empire period went a markedly increased concern for domestic comfort; house design and interior decoration began to occupy an increasingly important place in the lives of a much-expanded middle-class. Even the humiliating defeat in the Franco-Prussian War does not seem to have diverted the – above all Parisian – *bourgeoisie* from its pursuit of

the good life. Exteriors were expected to express the status and originality of house-owners, while interiors strove for effects of sumptuous opulence; even eminent cabinet-makers, such as Fourdinois, also described themselves as 'upholsterers' at the exhibition of 1867. Inevitably, the new shifts in taste were accompanied by the publication of lavish style books, both for architects and their clients. *Architecture Pittoresque et Moderne*, published *c.* 1870–75, was directed mainly towards property developers (*p. 166, except below left*). *Villas, Maisons de Ville et de Campagne* (*p. 166 below left and p. 167*) appeared in 1864; the authors were L. Leblanc and L. Isabey, Inspecteur des Palais Impériaux. Projects for individual room-settings abounded, such as these projects by A. Sandier (*p. 168*), dated 1891, in the collection of the Musée des Arts Décoratifs, Paris. *Habitations Particulières* (*p. 169*) by P. Planet was published in 1887. The

illustration is of a fashionable Parisian artist's drawing-room decorated in a style of overblown opulence to suggest the glories of the French Renaissance.

pages 170–171

Eclecticism, revivalism and pastiche in a variety of styles characterized French interior design in the latter part of the nineteenth century. 'Gothic' had made an appearance in the early part of the century in the form of the so-called *style troubadour*; by the eighteen-eighties it had become just one of many styles – from Renaissance to Louis-Seize – used by decorators to enliven the domestic interiors of their middle-class clientèle. This project for a Gothic dining-room by G. Félix Lenoir dates from 1889.

pages 172–173

This project for a conservatory is dated 1892 and signed Pizzagalli; the original is in the collection of the Bibliothèque Forney, Paris.

pages 174–175

The excavations at Pompeii were clearly the inspiration for this decorative scheme (*p. 174*), while the French interest in North Africa is reflected in the decoration of wall and door in this illustration (*p. 175*) from Georges Rémon's *Peinture Décorative*.

pages 176–177

Floral decoration in two different late nineteenth-century contexts: a textile design from Mulhouse by Fernand Schaub (*p. 176*) is strikingly paralleled by a vase design by Baccarat of similar date. Fernand Schaub (1860–*c.* 1902) was one of the most distinguished figures in the Mulhouse textile industry. He took over the management of his father's design business in 1888 and in addition designed furniture, clothing and wallpaper. The design of the Baccarat vase shows the distinct influence of the contemporary vogue for *japonisme* and already hints in the sinuous tendril forms at the curvilinear vocabulary of Art Nouveau.

pages 178–179

This page of pelmet designs (*p. 178*) is from a seventy-eight-plate trade catalogue of wares by Hourcq et Ithourburu, dated 1880, now in the collection of the Bibliothèque Forney, Paris. Of similar date is this plate (*p. 179*) from a catalogue of ornamental fittings for apartments by Roussel et Lavenroohère, also in the Bibliothèque Forney.

pages 180–181

The twin late nineteenth-century design themes of comfort and revivalism are amply illustrated in these two plates from contemporary style publications. *La Tenture Française* (*c.* 1900) (*p. 180*) offered a series of suggested arrangements for curtains and drapes drawn from a variety of historical styles, most notably Louis-Quinze and Louis-Seize. The *Journal de l'Industrie et des Arts Utiles* (*p. 181*) included suggestions for whole room-settings, including this example of opulent comfort.

pages 182–3 & 208

These pages are reproduced from the trade catalogue of the Maison Garnier which supplied all varieties of fittings for the apartments and houses of the most design-conscious middle-class of Europe. Every conceivable historical period and style were ransacked to provide the models for ornamental handles, window bolts and hasps, and door knobs for a clientèle obsessed with tradition. Only the light-fittings (*p. 208*) seem to indicate a real break with the past and look towards the graceful curvilinearity of Art Nouveau.

pages 184–185

More Second Empire eclecticism; these studies for wall decoration and columnar forms are by Pierre-Victor Galland and are dated 1864. They are now in the collection of the Musée des Arts Décoratifs, Paris.

pages 186–187

Possibly best known for his designs for the stations of the Paris Métro, Hector Guimard (1870–1942) was one of the most consistently inventive – and prolific – of all the Art Nouveau designers. His realized work is extensive, including architecture, furniture and objects, all characterized by a confident handling of sinuous line and the supple relationship of larger masses. These qualities are beautifully displayed in these two pencil and chalk sketches for vase mounts.

pages 188–189

The appointment of Théodore Deck as design director of the Sèvres porcelain manufactory heralded a new era of brilliant innovation at the company. Although Deck died in 1891, his reforms ensured an aggressive design policy which eventually saw the company embrace a particularly pleasing form of Art Nouveau, as in these two plate designs of 1905 by Jeanne Bugureau-Leroux. The company had already exhibited extensively at the Paris 1900 Exhibition to international acclaim.

pages 190–191

The name of Christofle first came to prominence in the mid nineteenth century as suppliers of tableware to Louis-Napoléon. Founded in 1830 mainly as a jewellery workshop, the company was eventually transformed by taking up the process of electroplating in 1842, originally patented in the United Kingdom by the Elkington company. From this point onwards the company arrived at that almost exclusively French solution to production – the combination of a studio-style aesthetic with industrial production. In 1876 a major factory was constructed in the Paris suburb of Saint-Denis and Christofle became, effectively, the suppliers of stylish, well-designed tableware of traditional form to the *bourgeoisie,* although its more adventurous pieces were already looking towards the design revolutions of the *fin-de-siècle.* The design for a silver-plated serving-dish illustrated here dates from 1880.

pages 192, & 198–9

The colour saturation which had characterized the Second Empire interior and, to an extent, that of the eighteen-eighties, gave way quite rapidly in the eighteen-nineties to a surprisingly modulated and understated palette, at least in the more sophisticated households. Textiles, wallpapers and interior woodwork appeared in pale pink, pale blue, light green and yellow. Typical of the new aesthetic were the designs published by Georges Rémon in *Intérieures Modernes (pp. 192 and 198),* c. 1895, which consisted of 60 plates *en pochoir.* The interiors are fully integrated; furniture and furnishings are clearly intended to complement the overall design of the room; curvilinear decoration is played discreetly over individual pieces and areas. Designs for individual doorways and wall treatments appeared in a slightly more organic version of Art Nouveau in the roughly contemporary *Menuiserie d'Art Nouveau (p. 199).*

page 193

The façade elevation of the Villa Flore by Hector Guimard; the designer is clearly as much at home in relating the more monumental masses of architecture to each other as in delineating the graceful forms of his domestic designs *(see pp. 186–187).*

pages 194–195

For the final decade of the nineteenth century and the first decade of the twentieth, the production of the Sèvres factory relied heavily on the design vocabulary of curvilinear Art Nouveau. This vase design of 1897 *(p. 195)* employs the vegetation decoration so characteristic of the movement, but with a force and clarity which lift the pattern out of the ordinary. Later, the factory started to produce wares in the Art Deco style, a faint trace of which can be discerned in these two clock designs *(p. 194)* of 1907 and 1911 respectively.

pages 196–197

The Baccarat company also turned to the floral motifs of high Art Nouveau for some of its production around 1900. Dating from 1899, this is one of two pencil and ink drawings in the company archives of the flowers and leaves of *Nepenthea mixta,* intended to form the etched decoration on the sides of a glass vase.

pages 200–201

The Baccarat archive, housed in the company factory, contains hundreds of original documents and records which trace the history of design and production from 1868 to the nineteen-thirties. Much of the archive consists of scrapbooks filled with immaculately drawn representations, some actual size, of each piece produced by the company during that period. These pages from a book containing designs for 1892–93, show carafes and stemmed glasses respectively.

pages 202–203 & 206–207

Further examples of the design repertory of the Sèvres factory ; these project sketches are part of a design for a seven-part coffee set. The company archive dates these pages *(pp. 202–203)* as December 1899. The vase designs *(pp. 206–207),* in high Art Nouveau form, are signed by Geneviève Rault and appear in the company records for 1900.

pages 204–205

Needless to say, the most adventurous aspects of late nineteenth-century design did not necessarily inform all aspects of the production of household goods and equipment. Many of the kitchen and garden artefacts produced for the now undoubtedly rich and powerful French middle-class retained traditional forms. These pages are taken from the richly varied trade catalogue of the Comptoir Français de Quincaillerie Rebattet et Cie, published in 1895. The catalogue forms part of a substantial collection held by the Bibliothèque Forney in Paris, which also includes catalogues from the main Paris department stores.

Art Deco and MODERNISM

The duality which emerged in the applied arts in the last two decades of the nineteenth century of a demand for comfortable revivalist styles coexisting with the preference of an élite clientèle for adventurous new design continued well into the first half of the twentieth century. In addition, several of the leading designers of the Art Nouveau period continued to create furniture and interiors in that style, even when the most adventurous of a new generation of designers were already working in the style which eventually came to be known as Art Deco. Other interesting divergences occurred. Manufacturers, for instance, were loathe to give up the lucrative business of making reproduction furniture, yet retailers in the form of the great department stores were quick to set up their own design studios to promote new fashions. René Guilleré, founder of the Société des Artistes-Décorateurs in 1901, joined the staff of Printemps in 1912. Later, Paul Follot established a studio for Bon Marché and Maurice Dufrène in 1921 created 'La Maîtrise' studio at the Galeries Lafayette to sell both stylish mass-produced furniture and custom-made pieces for wealthier patrons of the decorative arts.

Governmental backing for the new wave in design was important and the fact that it was forthcoming showed the tradition of centralized patronage of the decorative arts in France had not been lost. Important annual and bi-annual exhibitions were held at which the output of design studios and smaller workshops was accorded as much respect as that of larger industrial enterprises. The culmination of this public concern was, of course, the planning of a vast exhibition of the decorative arts for 1916, later postponed until 1922, and only finally taking place in 1925. There were private initiatives, too, such as the Salon d'Automne, founded by the Belgian-born Frantz Jourdain in 1903. The Salon was notable for displaying furniture in complete settings in its galleries. It also showed a new willingness to look outside France for inspiration and, in 1910, mounted an exhibition by members of the Munich Werkbund.

As well as that between revivalism and the new design, another divergence revealed itself at the exhibition of 1925 and in the years leading up to it: that between Art Deco and the rapidly growing group of Modernist designers. I have mentioned this duality in my introduction and examples of both styles are illustrated in this chapter. What is remarkable about the schemes for interiors in the style of Le Corbusier's Esprit Nouveau is the way in which the totality of an environment is realized through the inter-relationship of architectural elements, space, light, furniture and furnishings. Yet the two styles did not always remain distinct, as we can see in the work of Francis Jourdain (1876–1958). A designer of furniture and textiles, he oversaw the presentation of the smoking-room and gymnasium of the Ambassade Française at the 1925 Exposition. In spite of his connection with this prestigious temple of Art Deco, he went on to design inexpensive furniture for mass-manufacture.

Despite the reaction to Art Nouveau which was already becoming apparent by 1910 in the form of simpler lines and a stricter sense of proportion, the designers who were finally most closely associated with high Art Deco worked in luxury materials and in forms which sometimes recalled those of the Empire and Louis-Philippe periods. Rare woods and materials – ivory, sharkskin, Macassar ebony – characterized the works of Süe et Mare and of Ruhlmann. Unlike the Modernists, there could be no pretence here that any of these designs were for any other market than a wealthy élite. In one famous example of a sudden shift of taste, the wealthy *couturier* Jacques Doucet sold his collection of eighteenth-century furniture and objects to replace it with an equally sumptuous assembly of works by Paul Iribe, Marcel Coard, Pierre Legrain and Jean Dunand; his one gesture to Modernism was to include work by Eileen Gray.

It is the work of Jacques-Émile Ruhlmann (1879–1933), however, which can most appropriately form the end-note to this exploration of the French applied arts through original designs and published material. His *ateliers* in Paris in the nineteen-twenties provided a direct link to the central traditions of French design in their employment of specialist craftsmen and their concern for excellence in all aspects of their creations. Born in Paris, Ruhlmann began to design furniture in 1901 and by 1925 had become the most eminent *ébéniste* and *ensemblier* in the city. We illustrate here some of his original sketches which do give an intimate feeling of the master designer-craftsman at work. The forms of the pieces sometimes seemed to have been inspired by those of the Louis-Seize style, while others have a distinct air of Empire. His colour schemes also bespoke luxury and sensuousness: silver, grey, dark-brown and gold. And, lastly, in a poignant gesture towards the past of the tradition illustrated in this book, he marked his creations individually with an *estampille* in the manner of the eighteenth-century *ébénistes*.

pages 214-215
The spirit of the twentieth century; this practical yet stylish design for 'a young man's bedroom' unites the decorative elements of Art Deco with the utilitarianism of Modernism. It was originally published in *Suggestions d'Intérieurs Modernes* in the nineteen-twenties.

page 216
The art and craft of traditional glass-blowing; this photograph shows production at the Baccarat factory in the pre-World War I period. By 1908 the company employed some two thousand workers and had opened a special factory for the production of perfume bottles.

G.CHAMPION.

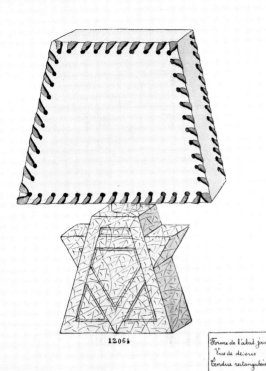

12064

Forme de l'abat-jour
Vue de dessus
Tendue rectangulaire

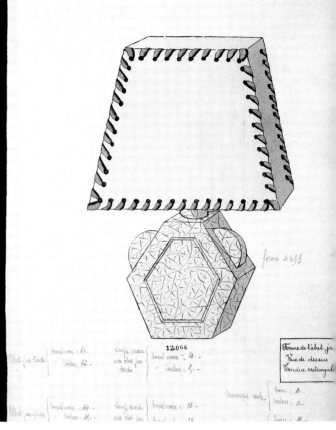

forme 4413

12066

Forme de l'abat-jour
Vue de dessus
Tendue rectangul

Abat jour tendu { Email ivoire = 61.
{ Couleurs = 62.

Lampe dessus { Email ivoire = 84. –
avec abat jour { Couleurs = 85. –
tendu

Céramique seule { Forme = 10.
{ Couleurs = 11.
{ Couleurs = 11.

Abat jour plissé { Email ivoire = 84.
{ Couleurs = 84.

Lampe dorée { Email ivoire = 88.
avec abat-jour {

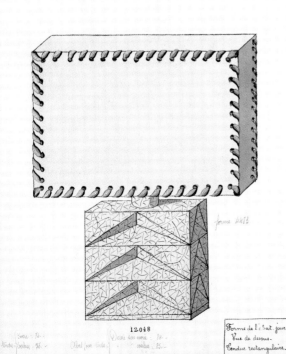

forme 4483

12048

Forme de l'abat-jour
Vue de dessus
Tendue rectangulaire.

{ ivoire = 74.
Tendue { Couleurs = 76.

{ Email ivoire = 74.
Abat jour tendu { couleurs = 78.

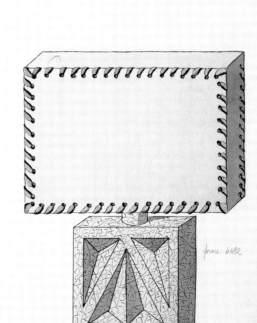

forme 4482

12047

Forme de l'abat-jour
Vue de dessus
Tendue rectangulaire.

Abat jour tendu { Ivoire bas ivoire = 80.
{ Avec bas couleurs = 85. –

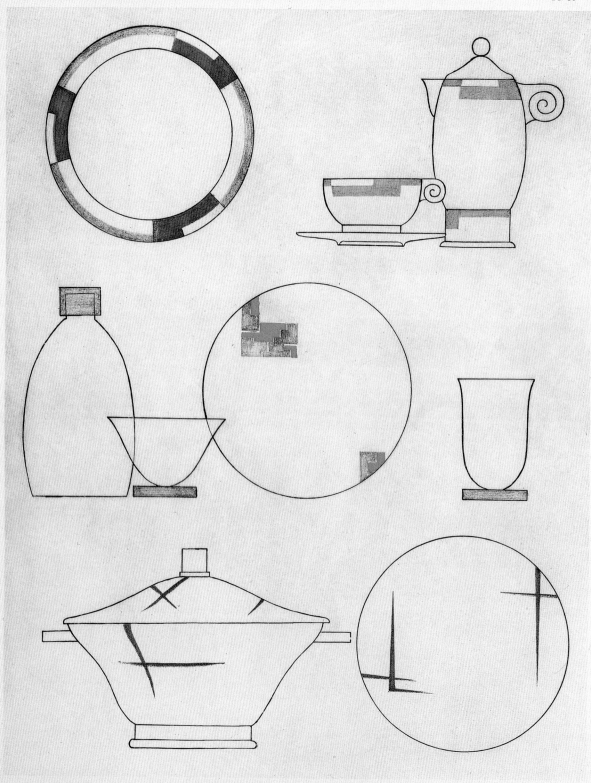

CÉRAMIQUE ET VERRERIE DE TABLE
par Jean Luce

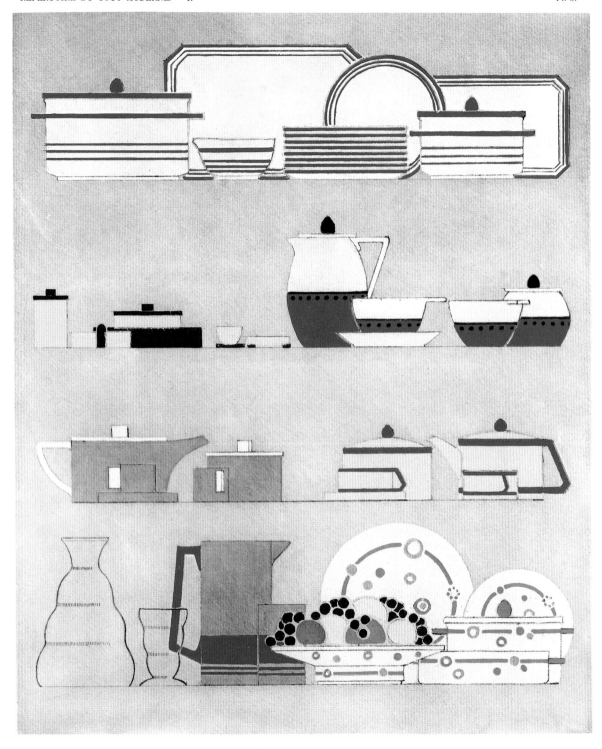

CÉRAMIQUES DE TABLE
Par Francis Jourdain

A.D.

224

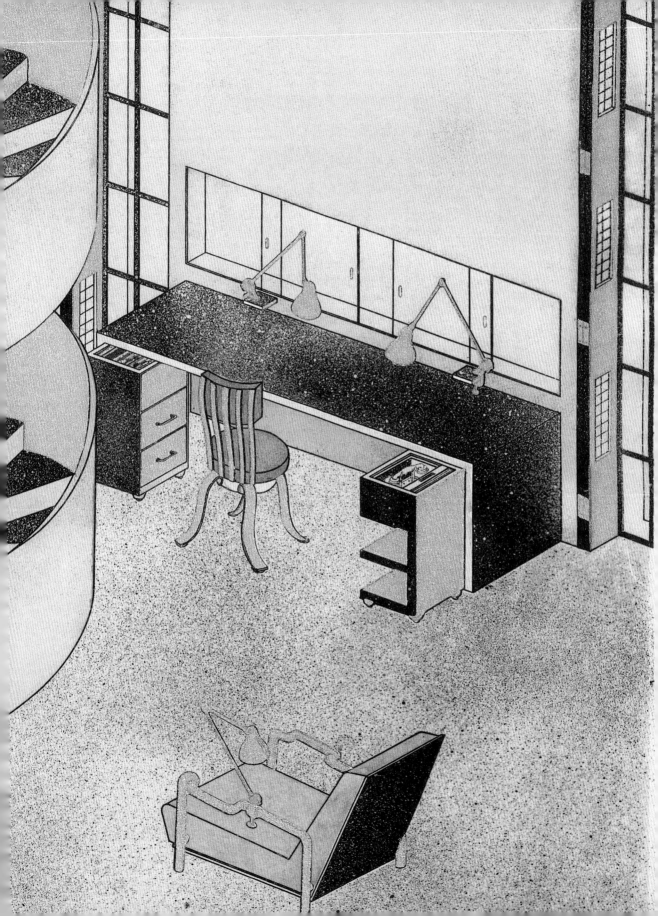

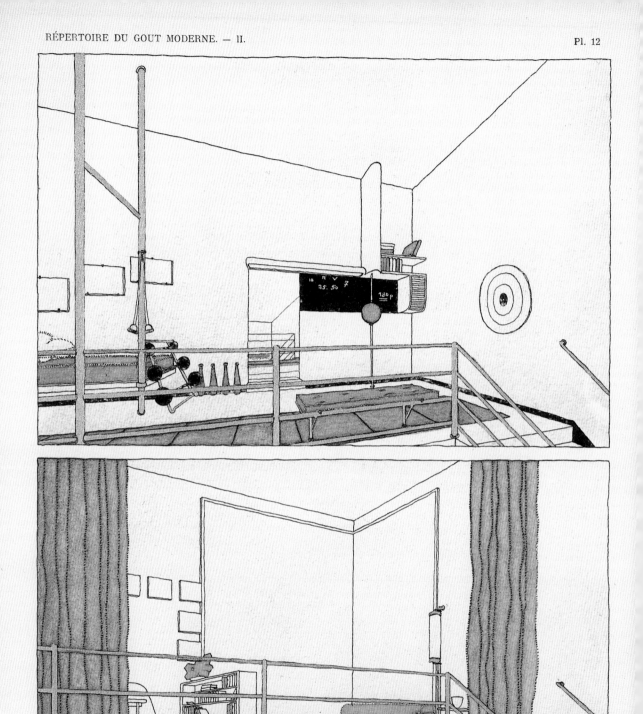

ATELIER-STUDIO
Galerie, par Maurice Matet

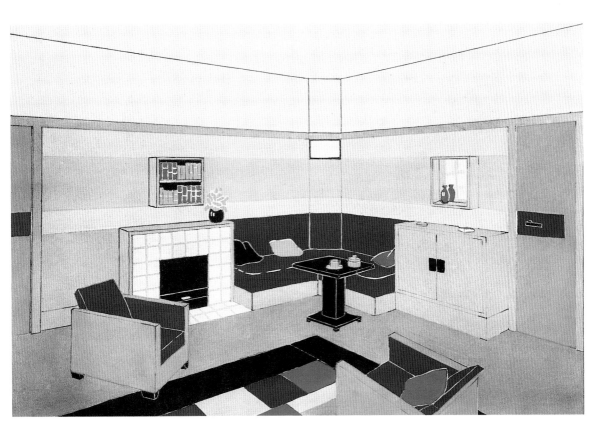

Pl. 40

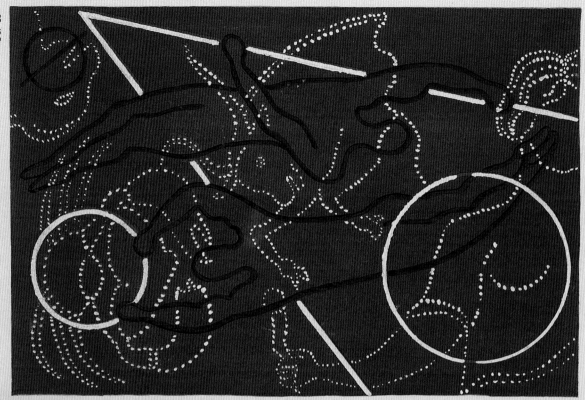

TAPIS

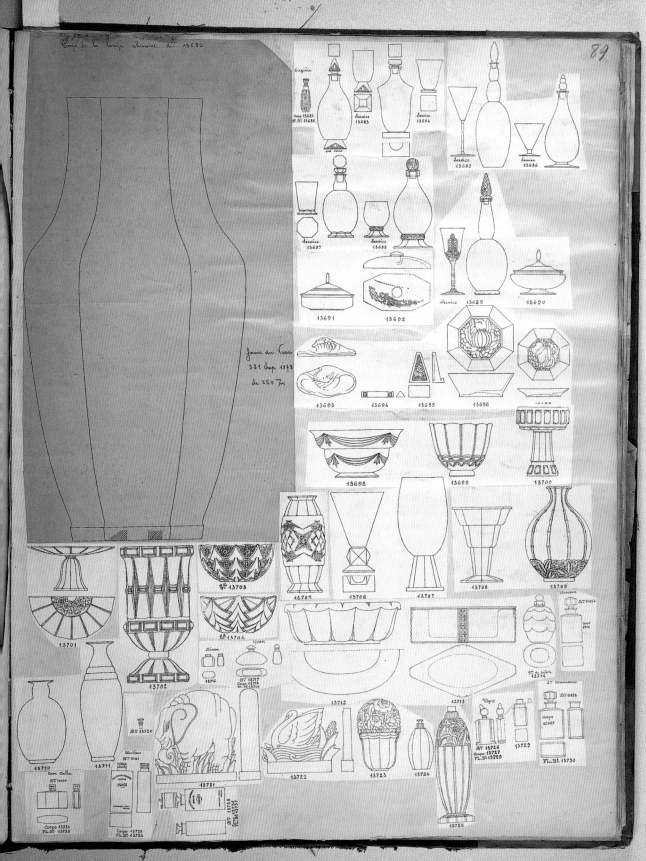

Vax Rapin n°15

Vax Rapin n°16

33 et 34 . 25

160

79

Vase Rupm n° 19
n° 30. 25

96 1

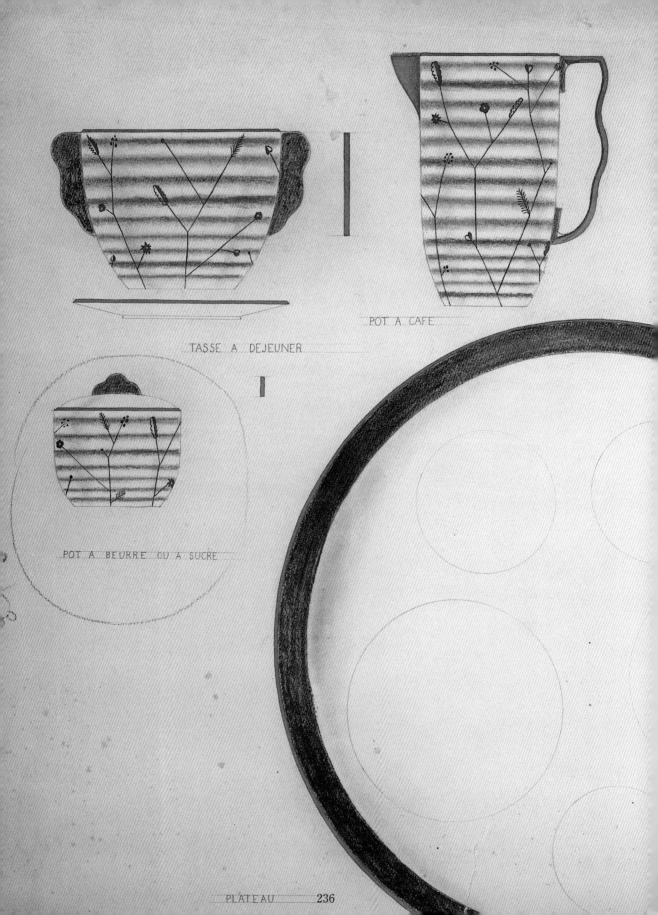

POT A CAFE

TASSE A DEJEUNER

POT A BEURRE OU A SUCRE

PLATEAU 236

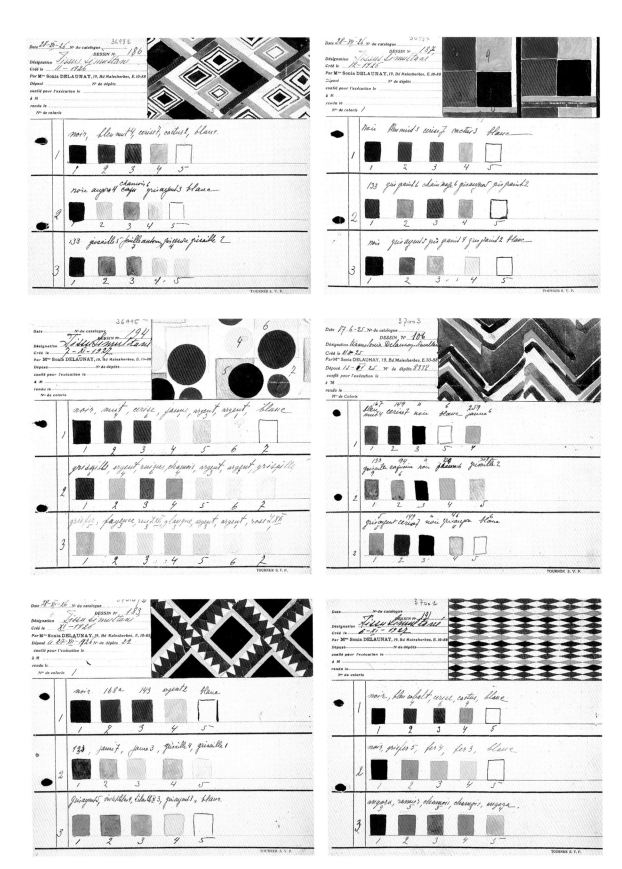

à compléter

ATELIER

marinot

239

TAPIS
par Da Silva Bruhns

Pl. 34

242

16,°10.2/

6

Art Deco and MODERNISM

Jacques-Émile Ruhlmann. Many of the designs have a hybrid quality, as we see the intermingling of Art Deco and Modernism as the decade advanced; this crossover effect is especially notable in the ceramics and glassware of Jean Luce and Francis Jourdain, both of whom participated in the great decorative arts exhibition of 1925. Interesting, too, are the designs of Jean-Charles Moreux, who clearly aligned himself with the Modernists before being seduced in the nineteen-thirties by classical revivalism. His *bureau-bibliothèque (pp. 226–227)* already shows some signs of whimsy in the forms of the chairs. Bruno da Silva Bruhns, who brought a kind of decorative Modernism to rug design, enjoyed an international reputation and cooperated with a number of other distinguished designers, including McKnight Kauffer. The *Répertoire* also published rug designs by Boberman.

lamp bases is taken from one of a dozen or so especially large scrapbooks in the Baccarat archives. As their form (especially that of the vases) indicates, most of the designs date from *c.* 1925 and include several by Georges Chevalier (1894–1987), one of a number of well-known independent designers who worked for Baccarat during the nineteen-twenties. About the same time Chevalier also designed the Pavillon Christofle/Baccarat for the Paris 1925 Exposition after a career with the company which had begun in 1916. A distinguished designer in other fields, Chevalier also worked with Léon Bakst on the set designs for Diaghilev's Ballets Russes.

6

Art Deco and MODERNISM

and high priest of the style, Jacques-Émile Ruhlmann, was invited to design a number of pieces. The stylistic preoccupations of the Sèvres design department can perhaps be seen more clearly in the decoration of the wares rather than in their shapes. The tableware of the period (*pp. 233 and 236*) shows a pleasantly light and whimsical touch in design. But the true ingenuity of the Sèvres designers is supremely illustrated in dozens of project drawings for vases (*pp. 234–235, 238*), in which the same basic shapes were used to produce very varied effects through the subtle use of different decorative schemes.

page 237

Sonia Delaunay (1885-1979) effectively revolutionized textile design during the nineteen-twenties. Her brightly coloured, geometrical patterns brought a painter's palette to an industry stifled by traditionalism. These colour cards are part of a collection of the artist's work held in the Musée des Tissus, Lyons.

page 239

Originally associated with the group of painters known as the 'Fauves', Maurice Marinot (1882–1962) is now best known for his work as a glass-maker. These designs (dated 1923–29) from sketches in the collection of the Musée des Arts Décoratifs, Paris, show his distinctive geometrical style, which was generally applied to ornamental ware, such as vases and bowls. Some of his finished work made use of 'accidental' characteristics in the form of crackling and bubbles, and would often be further decorated with etched figures.

pages 241–243

The taste of the twenties designers for geometrical effects was not confined to such individual artist-craftsmen as Marinot. Larger concerns, like Sèvres and Baccarat, catering for a much wider public, produced wares which, either in form or decoration, reflected this aspect of the Art Deco style – this was, after all, the Jazz Age. Baccarat was especially adventurous in its promotion of sculptural forms for a larger market; this sketch for a vase (*p. 241*) is taken from a pattern book of designs to be manufactured in 1935 in the company archive. As such, it must represent one of the last flings of the Deco style. The two urns from Sèvres (*pp. 142–243*), painted in black and white, achieve their effect through the brilliance of their decoration.

SELECT BIBLIOGRAPHY

Many of the volumes, records and documents from which the material reproduced in this book has been drawn are, by their very nature, unpublished and, in many cases, not immediately accessible. Indeed, the best possible bibliography for this book would be a complete listing of the archives and records held in public collections and individual companies throughout France. The titles listed below are of those books which I would recommend for further reading.

BACRI, Clotilde, *Daum*, London, 1993

BARON, Stanley and DAMASE, Jacques, *Sonia Delaunay*, London, 1995

CAMARD, Florence, *Ruhlmann: Master of Art Deco*, London, 1986

DAMASE, Jacques, *Sonia Delaunay Fashion and Fabrics*, London, 1997

DUNCAN, Alastair, *Art Deco Furniture*, London, 1992

DUNCAN, Alastair and de Bartha, Georges, *Glass by Gallé*, London, 1984

DUNCAN, Alastair, *Art Nouveau Furniture*, London, 1982

FRÉGNAC, Claude, *Les Styles Français*, Paris, 1975

HASLAM, Malcolm, *In the Nouveau Style*, London, 1989

HOSKINS, Lesley, *The Papered Wall*, London, 1994

LEBEAU, Caroline and Dirand, Patricia, *Fabrics: The Decorative Art of Textiles*, London, 1994

MARCILHIAC, Félix, *Jean Dunand*, London, 1991

MELLER, Susan and ELFFERS, Joost, *Textile Designs*, London, 1991

MOULIN, Pierre, LEVEC Pierre, DANNENBERG Linda, *Pierre Deux's French Country*, London, 1988

(ed.), *The Beaux-Arts and Nineteenth-Century French Architecture*, London, 1984

MIDDLETON, Robin (ed.), *The Beaux-Arts and Nineteenth-Century French Architecture*, London, 1984

MUSÉE DES ARTS DÉCORATIFS, Paris: *Botanique et Ornement*, Réunion des Musées Nationaux, Paris, 1992

MUSÉE DES ARTS DÉCORATIFS, Paris: *Le Carnet des Tasses*, Réunion des Musées Nationaux, Paris, 1992

MUSÉE DES ARTS DÉCORATIFS, Paris: *Bordures et Frises*, Réunion des Musées Nationaux, Paris, 1992

MUSÉE DES ARTS DÉCORATIFS, Paris: *Fleurs et Motifs*, Réunion des Musées Nationaux, Paris, 1992

SCOTT, Katie, *The Rococo Interior*, New Haven, 1995

SCOTT, Philippa, *The Book of Silk*, London, 1993

THORNTON, Peter, *Authentic Decor*, London, 1984

THORNTON, Peter, *Seventeenth-Century Interior Decoration in England, France and Holland*, New Haven, 1978

VELLAY, Marc and Frampton, Kenneth, *Pierre Chareau*, London, 1986

PICTURE CREDITS

INDEX

Author's
ACKNOWLEDGMENTS

This book is made up of fragments. Like a design paperchase, scraps of information have led me to extraordinary discoveries: a friend casually mentioning a company archive, a hunch about a source of old documents, a cutting I'd kept from a magazine. Sometimes these clues led to treasures, sometimes not. But whatever the outcome, many people contributed greatly to the organization of my quest.

Especial gratitude is due to Marie-Noël de Gary and Sonia Edard at the Musée des Arts Décoratifs in Paris; Anne-Claude Lelieur, Paule-Andreé Moselle and Dominique DeAngeli Cayol, at the Bibliothèque Forney, Paris; Tamara Préaud at the Musée de Sèvres; Jean-François Keller at the Musée de l'Impression sur Étoffes in Mulhouse; Astrid Guillermin and Evelyne Gaudry-Poitevin at the Musées de la Chambre de Commerce et d'Industrie de Lyon; Bernard Jacqué for his patience and knowledge at the Musée du Papier Peint in Rixheim. I am deeply indebted to Philip de Bay of the Stapleton Collection in London for making available to me his incredible photographic archive of French design documents. Of the many companies I contacted, particular thanks should go to Marie-Claire Precheur, Brigitte Bury, Pascaline Noack and Alphonse Gauberville at Baccarat; to Anne Gros in charge of the museum and archives at Christofle, and Jean-Pierre Deméry and Elizabeth Ferriol at Souleiado for giving us access to their incredible archive of fruitwood printing blocks in Tarascon.

A lot of people helped with ideas and snippets of information, for which I must thank Suzanne Slesin, Daniel Rozensztroch, Nello Renault, Newell Turner, Susan Campbell, Susan Collier, Alain Weill, Priscilla Carluccio, Christian Dorémus and Sophie Mortimer.

My very special thanks go to John Scott, for all his assistance and support, and to the three photographers: Marc Schwartz, who shot the preliminary page photographs at Souleiado; Jean-Louis Losi, for all the photographs of the Sèvres Museum documents, and Kulbir Thandi, for the contents page photograph.

First published in the United Kingdom in 1999 as *The French Archive of Design and Decoration*
by Thames & Hudson Ltd, 181A High Holborn, London WC1V 7QX

www.thamesandhudson.com

© 1999 and 2008 Thames & Hudson Ltd, London
French Style and Decoration: A Sourcebook of Original Designs

British Library Cataloguing-in-Publication Data
A catalogue record for this book is available from the British Library
ISBN 978-0-500-51400-9

Printed and bound in China by C & C Offset Printing Co. Ltd.

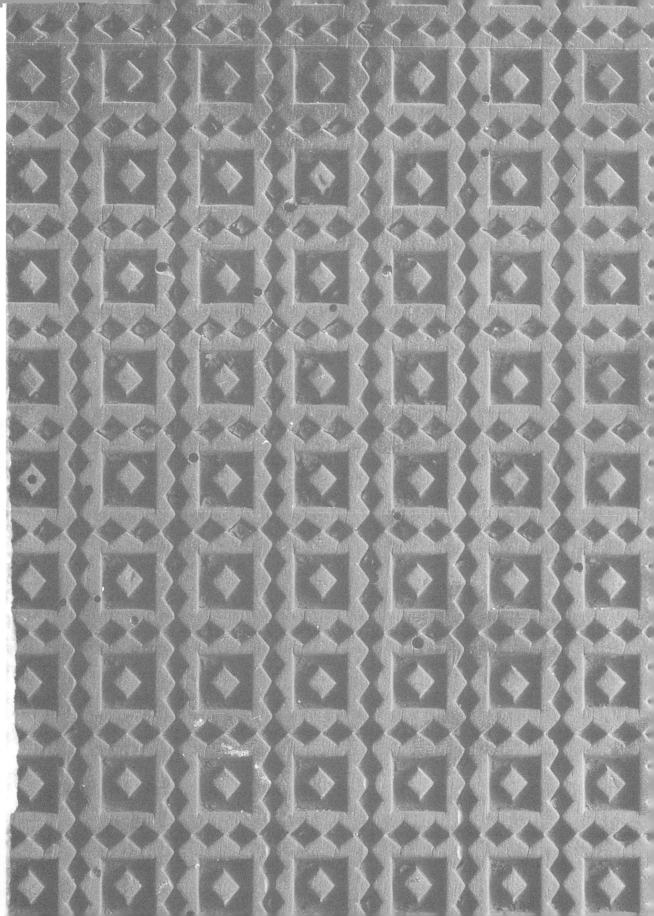